"may be correct" ♡

# History, Empathy and Conflict

Philip Towle

# History, Empathy and Conflict

Heroes, Victims and Victimisers

palgrave
macmillan

Philip Towle
POLIS
University of Cambridge
Cambridge, UK

ISBN 978-3-319-77958-4     ISBN 978-3-319-77959-1 (eBook)
https://doi.org/10.1007/978-3-319-77959-1

Library of Congress Control Number: 2018938662

© The Editor(s) (if applicable) and The Author(s) 2018
This work is subject to copyright. All rights are solely and exclusively licensed by the Publisher, whether the whole or part of the material is concerned, specifically the rights of translation, reprinting, reuse of illustrations, recitation, broadcasting, reproduction on microfilms or in any other physical way, and transmission or information storage and retrieval, electronic adaptation, computer software, or by similar or dissimilar methodology now known or hereafter developed.
The use of general descriptive names, registered names, trademarks, service marks, etc. in this publication does not imply, even in the absence of a specific statement, that such names are exempt from the relevant protective laws and regulations and therefore free for general use.
The publisher, the authors and the editors are safe to assume that the advice and information in this book are believed to be true and accurate at the date of publication. Neither the publisher nor the authors or the editors give a warranty, express or implied, with respect to the material contained herein or for any errors or omissions that may have been made. The publisher remains neutral with regard to jurisdictional claims in published maps and institutional affiliations.

Cover illustration: Pattern adapted from an Indian cotton print produced in the 19th century

Printed on acid-free paper

This Palgrave Pivot imprint is published by the registered company Springer International Publishing AG part of Springer Nature.
The registered company address is: Gewerbestrasse 11, 6330 Cham, Switzerland

*To Veronica who has been my support for the last 46 years*

# ACKNOWLEDGEMENTS

This book has benefitted greatly from the advice of friends and colleagues who devoted time and effort to reading my drafts, patiently answering my questions and recommending additional sources. In particular my thanks go to Christine Counsell, Peter and Ingrid Dixon, Ernest Gilman, Robert Jackson, John Kotch, James Mayall, Brendan Simms, Yoav Tenembaum, Simon Tustin and Arthur Williamson. It goes without saying that none of them is responsible for any single thing that I have written.

# Contents

1 Introduction 1

Part I Heroes to Victims 7

2 The Victimised 9

3 From Heroes to Victims 21

4 A Gratitude Free Zone 39

Part II Responses 49

5 'Memory Wars' and National Apologies 51

6 Historical Education 67

7 Restitution 77

Part III  Force and Memory                          85

8   From Heroes to Victimisers                      87

9   Memory as Guidance                              103

10  Hiding Victimisation                            115

11  2016: The Victory of Victimhood                 127

Bibliography                                        139

Index                                               155

CHAPTER 1

# Introduction

**Abstract** The Japanese proposal in 1978 that the anniversary of the nuclear attack on Hiroshima in August 1945 should be made the UN's World Peace Day showed how international culture had come to be dominated by the idea of victimisation. This has led since 1945 to a spate of national apologies which have gone some way to make amends for the sufferings of the past. But complaints about the past can be used to stir up antagonisms between nations and between national minorities and governments. They also remind us of the central importance of history and memory that determine national policies and how difficult it is to interpret them and put them in context.

**Keywords** Apologies • Glory • Hiroshima • History • Victims

The Japanese Ambassador proposed to the First United Nations (UN) Special Session on Disarmament in May and June 1978 that there should be a World Peace Day commemorating the anniversary of the nuclear attack on Hiroshima on 6 August 1945. On the face of it such a proposal made a good deal of sense. The immediate effects of the attack in terms of dead, maimed and dying were nightmarish and that event and the explosion over Nagasaki 3 days later are seen in Japan and amongst many elsewhere as uniquely dreadful. No wonder that they are lodged in memories, the image of the 'mushroom cloud' is ever present. The 1978 session was

© The Author(s) 2018
P. Towle, *History, Empathy and Conflict*,
https://doi.org/10.1007/978-3-319-77959-1_1

1

largely devoted to the threat posed by nuclear weapons and so the focus on Hiroshima was hardly out of place. But emphasis on victimhood divides people into victims and victimisers, and, in this case, ignored the context of the nuclear attacks. The explosions ended years of repression by the Japanese army in which hundreds of thousands of Chinese had died. In the rest of East Asia they ended a conflict that had killed thousands and reduced much of the region to a subsistence economy. For the United States and the other English-speaking countries they ended 4 years of brutal struggle.[1]

Pew, the respected US polling organisation exposed the continuing, though diminishing, nature of the disagreement in April 2015 when it asked Americans and Japanese about their attitudes towards the nuclear attacks. Of Americans polled, 56 % apparently believed that the attacks were justified compared with only 14 % of Japanese.[2] Pew pointed out that American support had declined from some 85 % in 1945 and that it was highest at 70 % amongst the over 65s against only 47 % of 18–29 year olds. The optimistic view is that this was because the taboo on the employment of nuclear weapons had grown stronger with the years as they have not been used in any subsequent conflict even when a country armed with such weapons was losing. An alternative explanation is that younger people are less familiar with the arguments for and against the use of nuclear weapons in 1945 and most particularly on whether or not Japan would have surrendered in any case and so whether or not the attacks saved lives. Fortunately, such controversies did not stop the two nations trusting each other in 2015 with 68 % of Americans trusting Japan and 75 % of Japanese trusting the United States. They had put the memories to one side so that normal life could continue.

The Japanese proposal at the UN in 1978 reflected wider issues than those involving nuclear weapons alone. It showed how modern societies were trying to come to terms with their memories. They had moved from a heroic to a victim culture, from one where 'great' men and women who protected their people or changed the world through war and the 'pursuit of glory' were the focus of admiration and commemoration to one where the emphasis was on sympathy for the ordinary men and women caught up in conflict and for youthful celebrities who died suddenly and unexpectedly. Some Western states, such as Britain and France, largely made this transition after the First World War but Japan preserved much of its ancient Samurai culture.[3] It raised an army of warriors to conquer China, drive the colonial powers out of East Asia and establish the Greater East

Asia Co-Prosperity Sphere. Its troops endured immense hardships in the Second World War and fought and died where they were ordered to stand.[4] As warriors they were beyond praise, as rulers they were abhorrent because they had been taught that human life was of little value and that their Emperor and nation were everything. In the Japanese religion of Shintoism or Emperor-worship they were the heroes of the hour yet, by 1978, many Japanese saw their predecessors, both uniformed and civilian, as the victims of that contest just as China, Malaya, the former Dutch East Indies and the Western allies regarded themselves as the victims of Japan's former heroes.

This book looks at the Japanese initiative and the other protests about historical victimisation which are so much a part of the contemporary international scene and which are unique in their prevalence and intensity to the modern world. Governments in the satisfied powers have often responded by making official apologies which try to reduce anger about the past. National leaders in the United States, Britain, Australia, New Zealand, France, Canada, Germany, Japan and elsewhere have all made such apologies as have leaders of some religious bodies including the Pope and the Methodist Church in Britain. This represents one of the most striking innovations in diplomatic practice over the last half century.

The book does not try to distinguish systematically between the ostensible motive for a policy and the 'actual' motive or the balance between the two. It assumes that states and their leaders act out of self-interest as well as emotion but that they stress national victimisation because they find it popular. Motives fluctuate from time to time and decision makers themselves may be unsure where the balance lies. No doubt Adolf Hitler felt that Germany had been badly treated by the Allies after the First World War but he also saw that complaints about such alleged victimisation were a popular cry that would help him to power.

Past events shape all our memories and in the modern world great numbers are for the first time aware of their country's history but have fitted only a fraction of it into their memory, a fraction chosen because it fits into their view of the world. Thanks to the media they are often also aware of recent wars however far away such wars may have been from their homeland. Many empathise with historic suffering as well as contemporary victims in other states. The first part of this book examines the origins of the 'age of victimhood' and the use which restless governments and movements make of this otherwise benevolent change to unite their people, denigrate other nations and justify their assertive foreign policy. The second part looks at national apologies, at the teaching of history and at the difficulties of making restitution to those peoples who were devastated in the past without creating yet further injustice and suffering.

The third part analyses the forceful response that powerful Western nations have made to what they see as victimisation in foreign countries. Governments intervene in foreign disputes to reduce the suffering and serve their national interests but national leaders, senior officers and journalists often know little of the history or culture of the disputants or the reasons for the conflict. These interventions have frequently ended in disasters with the interveners being blamed for increasing the numbers of victims. Past experience has to be used by all governments to guide their policies but it is their country's most recent and thus most vivid experiences that are lodged in memories rather than more distant events or the experience and culture of others. In any case each event is unique and historic analogies have to be used with great caution. Playing heroes or 'knights in shining armour' in an age of victimhood is inevitably a controversial exercise.

The last chapter brings the various themes together with an assessment of the impact they appear to be having on the world at the time of writing. In 2016 the victor in the US presidential elections appealed to the voters by presenting his country as the victim of recent history while the leaders of two other great powers, Russia and China have long described their countries as the victims of the Western powers or the Japanese. The fact that there are now three restless, great powers which favour changes in the status quo shows the power of cries of victimisation. It also raises serious concerns about international stability.

## Notes

1. For the suggestion that the use of nuclear weapons was unnecessary because Japan was ready to surrender see P. M. S. Blackett, *Military and Political Consequences of Atomic Energy*, Turnstile Press, London, 1948. For a critique of this viewpoint see Barton J. Bernstein, 'Compelling Japan's Surrender without the A-bomb, Soviet Entry or Invasion', *Journal of Strategic Studies*, June 1995. For a defence of the nuclear attacks see Paul Fussell, *Killing in Verse and Prose and Other Essays*, Bellew, London, 1988, pp. 13–37. Fussell, later Professor of Literature at the University of Pennsylvania, would have served in one of the invading forces had these been ordered to attack. For a classic analysis of the ferocious nature of the

war in the Pacific see John Dower, *War Without Mercy: Race and Power in the Pacific War*, Faber and Faber, London, 1986.
2. 'Americans, Japanese mutual respect 70 years after the end of World War 11', Pew Research Center, 7 April 2015. I quote opinion polls extensively in what follows although I accept that their accuracy may vary. I could have inserted qualifications such as 'apparently' or 'seemed to' on every occasion but that would have simply burdened the text. Whatever the criticisms of such polls they are preferable to the anecdotal evidence on which a commentator would otherwise have to rely. Analyses of opinion nowadays, however insightful, which do not use such polls, seem curiously anachronistic.
3. Walter A Skya, *Japan's Holy War: The Ideology of Radical Shinto Ultranationalism*, Duke University Press, Durham, 2009.
4. Fergal Keane, *Road of Bones: The Siege of Kohima 1944*, Harper, London, 2010, pp. 107–108, 318, 151–155; Srinath Raghavan, *India's War: The Making of Modern India 1939–1945*, Penguin Books, London, 2016, pp. 410–434.

# PART I

# Heroes to Victims

CHAPTER 2

# The Victimised

**Abstract** Almost all nations have been the victims of others at one time or another. The nationalist movements that grew up with industrialisation and mass education in the nineteenth century fed on stories of their ancestors' suffering. They freed the Balkans from Ottoman control but their anger has continued to tear the area apart down to the collapse of Yugoslavia. Nationalist movements played a major part in causing the two World Wars and they still continue to threaten the unity of Spain, the United Kingdom and other countries. Historical resentments add to the ferment in the Muslim world and cause bitter arguments between China, Japan, Taiwan and South Korea over the history of the Second World War.

**Keywords** Knowledge • Media • Nationalism • Religion • Victims

It would be a lucky nation indeed that had never had to struggle to survive in the face of genocidal attacks from other groups. Warriors were the great heroes because they alone stood between a people and massacre or a lifetime of slavery. Fortunately, most of their battles have been forgotten or have disappeared into the relatively unemotional pages of the history books. One historian employing genetic data has suggested that Viking raiders obliterated the Picts living in the Scottish Western isles and that there are now more descendants of the Picts living in Scandanavia than Scotland suggesting the people were either killed or carried away as slaves.[1]

© The Author(s) 2018
P. Towle, *History, Empathy and Conflict*,
https://doi.org/10.1007/978-3-319-77959-1_2

The land now occupied by the English was overrun in turn by the Romans, the Anglo-Saxons, the Danes and the Normans. The indigenous people were killed, absorbed by the invading culture or driven into the hills of Wales. The residue was dominated for centuries by the Norman elite. However, these disasters have long since been overtaken by later events that have made the English a satisfied nation generally happy with the aspects of their history which are most firmly lodged in their memories.[3]

Elsewhere the suffering has been much more recent or has left enduring scars. The *Old Testament* is quite largely a recital of the Jewish people's struggle against enslavement, brutality and destruction. The experience has been cemented in the national memory both by these sacred books and by the Jews' experience of persecution over the centuries. On other continents nomadic peoples, including the indigenous inhabitants of Australia, New Zealand and the Americas were simply overwhelmed by foreign intruders who settled on their lands. The native North Americans, Australians and others are only gradually finding their voices and struggling to make their sufferings understood.[2] Similarly, the scars of the Atlantic slave trade have been kept alive by the intensity of the trauma that has been passed down from generation to generation amongst the slaves' descendants.

Many peoples have been victim and victimiser at different periods. Thus, great civilisations such as Mesopotamia, India, Egypt, China or Iran, which once ruled vast empires, were later dominated by European intruders. When they recovered their strength their publics show the extent of their resentment over the past, and their governments and opinion formers often encourage this tendency to unite the nation. Anger at their humiliation by the European imperialists or the Japanese over the last 200 years has consequently left a deep impression on the foreign and security policies of the Chinese, the Indians, the Arab nations and Iranians.[3] When popular resentments about the past are combined with current power such nations are tempted to rectify past wrongs by force. The public opinion that their governments have helped to create constricts their ability to compromise. The full implications will take decades to work themselves out but all former colonies tend to be sensitive to foreign interference or criticism of their policies. In a 2014 poll the majority of Pakistanis said that US administrations should not even comment on their country's internal problems.[4] Such states stand now where Japan stood in the first half of the twentieth century after years of humiliation at the hands of the Americans and Europeans. They have to decide whether their historic resentments will lead them down the same path towards confrontation with their neighbours and the status quo powers which, in turn, have to deal with their sensitivity and their urge for change.

Thus, the seventieth anniversary of the end of the Second World War in 2015 proved as much a source of controversy as a celebration in East Asia. In Taiwan ex-President Lee Teng-hui, the former leader of the Kuomintang (KMT) Party, infuriated many when he told a Japanese journal that he had been proud to fight for Japan during the war and that he saw Japan as his fatherland. The head of the KMT's Central Policy Committee said that he should be harshly denounced and a party representative suggested that the KMT would introduce legislation to remove Lee's pension.[5] The Taiwanese President Ma Ying-jeou said that Taiwanese had always struggled *against* Japan after the Japanese conquered their island in 1895. The KMT was clearly determined to distance itself from Lee because an election was pending but its difficulties were compounded when another KMT member and a former Vice-President, Lien Chan attended China's victory parade on 3 September 2015. Chan wanted his visit to heal the rifts between Taiwan and the mainland but many Taiwanese felt he was participating in a celebration that distorted history by pretending that it was the communists who had played the more significant role in the defeat of Japan in 1945. On the other hand, the general Taiwanese view is that it was a Nationalist or Kuomintang victory. Memory and contemporary international politics collided.

They also clashed in Japan itself. Japanese leaders reflected the near consensus in their country by focusing on the bombing of Hiroshima and Nagasaki. In their view this makes them victimised rather than victimisers. Thus, consciously or unconsciously, they tried to turn attention away from the fact that Japan had precipitated the suffering in the first place by attacking and repressing Manchuria in 1931, followed by China proper from 1937 and finally the rest of East Asia. The Japanese Prime Minister, Shinzo Abe also appeared to excuse his country's behaviour by suggesting that Japan had to conquer other lands because it was unable to export its manufactures or find raw materials during the Great Depression of the 1930s. This and the growth of the Japanese population and the infertility of their islands were indeed the explanations the Japanese military deployed in the 1930s for their expansive policies. But, as observers pointed out at the time, their industry was so robust and the yen was pegged to the pound at such a low rate that it recovered very quickly from the worldwide economic difficulties. While poor Japanese suffered terribly, between

1931 and 1936 exports more than doubled from under 1200 million yen to nearly 2800 million.[6] The British found it impossible to protect both the Lancashire cotton industry and the interests of their Indian Empire in the face of Japanese exports and it was Lancashire that they sacrificed.[7] What destroyed Japanese trade in the long run was the country's aggressive foreign policy which led to the devastation of the East Asian economy during the Second World War.[8]

The development of mass societies through urbanisation, universal education and the spread of the media produce such historic claims and counter-claims of victimisation. During the period of modernisation many people move to the cities, crops are no longer directly relevant and their contact with immediate neighbours is often looser and more episodic. Instead they identify with their linguistic or social group and in previously troubled areas are encouraged by opinion formers to lodge certain events in their memories and complain about what happened at the hands of the imperialists and the lands 'they lost' to other peoples. In industrial cities they are similarly exhorted by radicals to protest the victimisation of their class by their employers. Consciously and unconsciously they now locate themselves both geographically and in the flow of history which suddenly seem vitally important to them. In the modern world the movement of people is vast and growing and the flow of information brings ever more awareness; everybody can now take an interest in political events because they try to force themselves on most via the radio or television; people do not have to be literate.[9] The villagers in remote areas of Nigeria or Brazil may be influenced by distant happenings or novel ideas, they may identify emotionally with the sufferings of people, however far away, who have the same religion, economic position or cultural identity as themselves.

While our rural ancestors thus knew a great deal about crops, animals and the effects of weather, we are superficially aware of a much wider range of subjects and are, probably at best, experts on a range no broader than our predecessors' competence. We have to close our mind to many issues because no one could remember the mass of facts and ideas available, a narrowing that increases with age. Polls show that, however educated people are and however well informed they would claim to be, very few have the names of many of the people whose doings are bandied around in the media impressed in their memories. In a February 2013 poll 90 % or more Britons failed to name the President of the European Council, the Secretary General of NATO, the Director of the International Monetary Fund or the President of Brazil. Admittedly more than half could name the President of Russia and the Chancellor of Germany but they had ignored the other names when they heard or read about them because they did not consider them so important to their lives.[10] There were only tiny differences between the various social grades or age groups in their knowledge of such facts. A survey carried out in 1988 amongst Members of the British Parliament showed that 'parking' information not immediately relevant extended in this highly politicised group beyond names to security policies; few knew what percentage of the gross national product was spent on defence or on Britain's nuclear force.[11]

The danger with the way in which we filter knowledge is clear. We select the facts that we need and can fit into a simplified historical pattern, and past victimisation is emotionally appealing to many people and regarded as useful by some governments and political parties. The Chinese government tries to divert attention from the tens of millions who died as a result of Mao Tse Dong's demonic schemes in the 1950s and 1960s by focusing attention on the Japanese invasion of their country in the 1930s.[12] Similarly in the nineteenth century the historic resentments stoked by radical nationalists led to conflict and tension at the very moment when industrialisation and trade should have been pulling the nations together. The advocates of free trade or the abolition of trade barriers between the nations, who argued that the resulting economic links would prevent war, proved sadly mistaken.

What occurred was like a flood spreading through a parched desert with trickles of water passing through tiny creeks and expanding into a great torrent. There was then a burgeoning of independence movements in the Turkish and Habsburg Empires, in Britain and in Russia. This new nationalism was to lead to a reconfiguring of the map of Europe and a century of warfare from 1848 to 1945. Hatreds were most destructive where the past had been most violent such as Eastern Europe and the Balkans. *The Times* complained during one of the wars tearing the Balkans apart of 'the wholesale massacre of the male population, the women and children abandoned to the savagery of the soldiers, the deliberate destruction of all appliances for shelter and food, so as to make the existence of the population who escape massacre almost impossible, the wounded killed after the battle is over'.[13] It was the assassination of the Austrian Archduke Franz Ferdinand by Serb nationalists which precipitated the First World War and the Nazi-Soviet pact to divide Poland which finally undermined the uneasy peace that had prevailed in Europe since Adolf Hitler came to power. After the millennium, the collapse of Yugoslavia and then the civil war in the Ukraine caused hundreds of deaths and deeply troubled international relations.

Throughout the twentieth century and beyond writers continued to chronicle the bitter historic feuds that plagued the Balkans. When the British novelist, Rebecca West toured Yugoslavia in the 1930s the debate amongst the inhabitants was whether their Turk, Venetian or Austrian conquerors were most to blame for what some of the educated saw as their own barbarism.[14] The memory of their independent status before these invasions and of their 'wealth and culture had been kept alive among the peasants, partly by the Orthodox Church which very properly never ceased to remind them that they had once formed a free and Christian state, and also by the national ballads'.[15] Nineteenth-century communications and education gave extra energy to these memories and, even where Muslims and Christians had lived in harmony for decades, old enmities were revived. Thirty years later the Yugoslav writer and political activist, Milovan Djilas described the hatred between the various Balkan peoples and how, when opportunity offered in the past, Montenegrins attacked Muslims 'because they were of an alien-Turkish-faith and a pillar of Turkish power through long centuries of Turkish enslavement'. Djilas said they felt 'a deep inner pleasure at attacking an alien faith with which a struggle to the death had constituted a historic way of life and thought'.[16]

Half a century later still the American journalist, Robert Kaplan's *Balkan Ghosts* showed how past sufferings and defeats continued to cause tension and conflict.[17] When Yugoslavia collapsed at around that time the Western powers intervened primarily because they sympathised with the victims; a decision and caste of mind which will be discussed repeatedly in the pages which follow. They hoped to restore order and protect the Muslim Bosniaks because they regarded both religious tension and historic anger as barbaric and irrational relics from another age. Relics indeed they were but to ignore their continuing power when stirred by opinion formers is to misunderstand the modern world. As an analyst of such victims put it, 'the mental representation of the historical drama and how it has been internalised remains in the minds of the members of that society and perpetuates their preoccupation with such representations whenever a new difficult situation arises.'[18]

It was much the same on the British periphery. Irish and Scottish nationalist leaders wanted their people to feel anger at the suffering of their ancestors at English hands. Within a few decades of their introduction, mass education and the consequent politicisation led to the independence of Ireland where nationalists recalled that the English landowners had killed or dispossessed their forbears. Such patriots argued that their culture, religion, language and interests could only be protected by independence. Politicians in Westminster hoped that by making economic concessions they could win over the bulk of Irish people but the outbreak of a nationalist insurgency after the First World War showed that past suffering could not be so easily forgiven. Contrary to Marxist claims, economics provides a weak motive when compared with current and historic resentments and religious differences otherwise no country would tear itself apart and destroy its own cities in civil war and violence.

David Thomson, the BBC radio producer and writer explained Irish feelings in his sensitive study of the time he spent on a small estate owned by Protestants in Ireland in the 1920s. There the Irish people 'secretly cherished hatred for the [English] Major, their present landlord and employer whom in day to day relationships they loved-cherished this hatred because of his ancestors and theirs, and because it might help their advancement.' Although they lived side by side in Ireland the ignorance of the English and the Irish of each other's culture was considerable, and the English found it difficult to understand Irish grudges because English texts skated over the history of Anglo-Irish relations.[19]

The potato famine of the 1840s was the pivotal incident in modern Anglo-Irish relations because it was so horrific, because it occurred just when Irish people were becoming more aware of what was happening and because survivors could flee to the United States where they formed a powerful anti-English minority. There has been argument ever since about how much of the starvation was due to the rulers' incompetence or to the ideology of Charles Trevelyan and his colleagues in London. A former government official in India, he was the bureaucrat in charge of the British response under the Whig government led by Lord John Russell which was in power for the later and worst period of the famine. Trevelyan believed that he should maintain tight control over aid to prevent corruption and that Ireland needed to go through an agricultural revolution similar to the one which had taken place in England during the seventeenth and eighteeth centuries where enclosures of land displaced village labourers.[20] But in England the enclosures forced the displaced labourers to move to the developing industrial cities. In Ireland the short-term result was the starvation of perhaps a million people and the forced emigration of a million others. The long-term consequence was the destruction of the British-Irish state and the emergence of groups in North America and elsewhere bitterly hostile to the English. According to the Irish politician and writer, Conor Cruise O'Brien, 'many Irish-Americans became more anti-English than were many Irishmen who remained in Ireland'.[21] In Thomson's view, older Irish people regarded the potato famine of the 1840s as an 'act of God'; 'cut off from public information, supported only by religious faith, they could not have known [what happened]. But the politically informed did know and the truth soon spread urged on by a rapid growth in literacy, so much so that English policy during the famine and for seventy years afterwards created ill-feelings between the two nations more bitter or at least more generally felt than any that had gone before'.[22]

Some of the promises made by the nationalist leaders were unrealised after independence. Irish literature arguably reached its apogee in the period beforehand and the use of the Gaelic language continued to decline despite intensive efforts in the schools.[23] On the other hand, polls carried out in 1981 and 1990 showed that Irish people were particularly proud of their country. Of the Irish, 76 % expressed such views against 17 % in West Germany, 41 % in Italy and 52 % in Britain.[24] In Northern Ireland Catholic nationalist anger over past suffering and current poverty was fierce enough to inspire the IRA campaign in the province in the 1970s and 1980s which led to the deaths of over 3000 people, equivalent to tens of thousands of deaths in the United Kingdom as a whole.[25] Typically for an area with a troubled history, even after the Good Friday Agreement brought a measure of stability in April 1998, polls showed that some people in the area were sympathetic to paramilitary organisations of both denominations. Because of the centuries of repression, toleration of community violence as a way of protest was thus considerable.[26]

In the twentieth century the Scots also focused on history, and nationalist politicians encouraged them to implant past victimisation in the national memory. This contrasts with the situation a century before when the Scottish geologist and folklore expert, Hugh Miller congratulated both countries for coming together through agreement rather than conquest. As an evangelical Christian he felt that the greatest difference between the two countries was in the intense Scottish interest in theology and boasted to a group of Englishmen, 'it has done for our people what all your Societies for the Diffusion of Useful Knowledge, and all your Penny and Saturday Magazines will never do for yours; it has awakened their intellects, and taught them how to think'.[27] A century later, Moray McLaren the Scottish travel writer, civil servant and BBC editor, stressed memory rather than religion as the focus of Scottish interest and distinction from the English:

Scots are constantly being surprised by the readiness with which we all, even the most prosaic of us, lean upon our past, the eagerness with which we refer to it and the passion with which we disagree about it. The English who, though they are our nearest neighbours, are in many respects more distant from us than those more geographically distant, are the most surprised by this trait in us. They readily admit that we are, above everything else, a country of individuals and therefore prone to disputatiousness. But why dispute about the past? What is the good of it?[28]

Mass education, the decline of religious faith and the discovery of North Sea oil encouraged the growth of the Scottish National Party which wanted the two countries to separate.[29] Once again the English tried to placate the protesters with concessions leading eventually to the establishment of a separate parliament in Edinburgh and to a referendum on independence in 2015. The English were blamed for the country's ills and though independence was rejected by a 10 % majority the campaign had created deep divisions in the society and the Scottish National Party won all but three seats in the May 2015 general election.

Nevertheless, elsewhere at the start of the twenty-first century it was often religious as much as national history which fostered tension. The radical Muslims or Islamists' justifications for acts of terror, such as the 9/11 attacks on New York and Washington, have been a mixture of contemporary politics and more distant history. They objected to the presence of US troops in Saudi Arabia and Western interference in wars between or inside Muslim states such as the Kuwaiti–Iraq War of 1990 or the civil war in Libya in 2011. They also protested the historic part that the West has played in establishing and then supporting Israel. They were antagonised by the infiltration of Muslim societies by Western culture through films, television and tourism and they claimed that the West has been the enemy of Islam since the Crusades in the Middle Ages. Yet, from the Western point of view, it was Islam which was on the offensive against the West for the best part of a millennium and the Crusades were justified in part as a way of repulsing the Muslim attacks on Byzantium. Each civilisation spasmodically regarded the other as the enemy and its own people as the victims.[30]

Many, perhaps most, of the complaints of historic suffering are true or partially true, very often the treatment of the victims was appalling by modern standards, but the degree to which they are true is not the issue here.[31] Anger over the sufferings of a group's ancestors increases its cohesion and diminishes or depersonalises the victimisers' descendants. It can be an effective rallying cry and it may camouflage the growing power of the state or group which burnishes its suffering. The combination of great power and anger can undermine international stability. The anger of national minorities can threaten domestic stability, anger against national minorities can lead to massacres or can encourage foreign powers to intervene in ways which sometimes exacerbate conflicts. Past victimisation can spawn further suffering.

## Notes

1. Alistair Moffat, *The British: A Genetic Journey*, Virlinn, Edinburgh, 2013, pp. 204–205.
2. Elizabeth Furniss, *The Burden of History: Colonialism and the Frontier Myth in a Rural Canadian Community*, UBC Press, Vancouver, 1999.
3. Henry Hardy, Editor, Isaiah Berlin, *The Crooked Timber of Humanity: Chapters in the History of Ideas*, Pimlico, London, 2013, pp. 267–268. Manharsin, Chatterjee Miller, *Wronged by Empire: Post-Imperial Ideology and Foreign Policy in India and China*, Stanford University Press, Stanford, 2013. Aaron L. Friedberg, 'Globalisation and Chinese grand strategy', *Survival*, February–March 2018.
4. Gallup Pakistan Weekly Cyberletter, 22 September 2014, Gilani Research Foundation.
5. 'Lee Teng-hui's benefits as ex-president may be stripped', China News Agency, 21 August 2015; 'Lien's attendance of China's WWII anniversary parade improper' China News Agency, 29 August 2019; 'Controversy over Lien's presence at WWII parade in Beijing lingers', China News Agency, 4 September 2015.
6. Tota Ishimaru, *Japan Must Fight Britain*, Paternoster Library, London, 1936; William Henry Chamberlain, *Japan over Asia*, Duckworth, London, 1938, p. 172.
7. Naoto Kagotani, 'Japan's commercial penetration into British India', in Philip Towle and Nobuko Margaret Kosuge, Editors, *Britain and Japan in the Twentieth Century*, I. B. Tauris, London, 2007, pp. 62–81.
8. Paul Einzig, *The Japanese "New Order" in Asia*, Macmillan, London, 1943; Mark Parillo, *The Japanese Merchant Marine in World War II*, Naval Institute Press, Annapolis, 1993; Mark Harrison, *The Economics of World War II*, Cambridge University Press, Cambridge, 1998.
9. For a classic study of the change in the Middle East see Daniel Lerner, *The Passing of Traditional Society*, Free Press, Glencoe, 1958.
10. YouGov Survey, 27–29 January and 3–4 February 2013.

11. *MPs and Defence: A Survey of Parliamentary Knowledge and Opinion*, Institute for European Defence and Strategic Studies, London, 1988, tables 7 and 8.
12. For the Sino-Japanese war see Rana Mitter, *China's War with Japan: The Struggle for Survival 1937–1945*, Penguin, London, 2014; for Mao's impact see Frank Dikotter, *Mao's Great Famine: The History of China's Most Devastating Catastrophe 1958–1962*, Bloomsbury, London, 2011.
13. 'Neutral Europe cannot shut its eyes', *The Times*, 3 September 1877.
14. Rebecca West, *Black Lamb and Grey Falcon: A Journey through Yugoslavia*, Macmillan, London, 1955.
15. West, *Black Lamb*, p. 519.
16. Milovan Djilas, *Land without Justice: An Autobiography of his Youth*, Methuen, London, 1958, p. 90.
17. Robert D. Kaplan, *Balkan Ghosts: A Journey Through History*, St Martin's Press, New York, 1993. For the ensuing controversy see Timothy Garton Ash, 'Bosnia in Our Future', *New York Review of Books*, 21 December 1995; Robert D. Kaplan reply to Timothy Garton Ash, *New York Review of Books*, 21 March 1996.
18. V. D. Volkan in Gobodo-Madikizela and Van Der Merwe, Editors, *Memory, Narrative and Forgiveness*, Cambridge Scholars, Newcastle, p. 10.
19. David Thomson, *Woodbrook*, Penguin, Harmondsworth, 1976, pp. 10, 26 and 71. In contrast see Dean William Inge, *England*, Hodder and Stoughton, London, 1938, p. 66, 'An Englishman is simply unable to comprehend the brooding hatred of the Irishman, which has no better ground than that Cromwell exercised the laws of war somewhat severely against the Irish rebels, and that William III won the battle of the Boyne'.
20. Enda Delaney, *The Curse of Reason: The Great Irish Famine*, Gill and Macmillan, Dublin, 2012.
21. Conor Cruise O'Brien, *States of Ireland*, Hutchinson, London, 1972, pp. 43–44.
22. Thomson, *Woodbrook*, p. 181.
23. F. S. L. Lyons, *Culture and Anarchy in Ireland*, Clarendon Press, Oxford, 1979, chapter six; John Hutchinson, *The Dynamics of Cultural Nationalism: The Gaelic Revival and the Creation of the Irish National State*, Allen and Unwin, London, 1987.
24. Sheena Ashford and Noel Timms, *What Europe Thinks: A Study of Western European Values*, Dartmouth, Aldershot, 1992, p. 90.
25. Bernadotte C. Hayes and Ian McAllister, 'Public support for political violence and paramilitaries in Northern Ireland and the Republic of Ireland', *Terrorism and Political Violence*, 2005, 17, 599–617.
26. Hayes and McAllister, 'Public support', p. 607.

27. Hugh Miller, *First Impressions of England and Its People*, William P. Nimmo, Edinburgh, 1869, pp. 3, 4 and 10.
28. Moray McLaren, *The Scots*, Penguin, Harmondsworth, 1951, p. 8. For a brief history of the union between the two countries see Richard Pares, 'A quarter of a millennium of Anglo-Scottish Union', in Bernard Pares, *The Historian's Business and Other Essays*, Clarendon, Oxford, 1961, 84–99.
29. 'How education makes people less religious—and less superstitious too', *The Economist*, 11 October 2014, p. 73.
30. Richard Fletcher, *The Cross and the Crescent: Christianity and Islam from Muhammad to the Reformation*, Viking, New York, 2004: Bernard Lewis, *From Babel to Dragomans: Interpreting the Middle East*, Weidenfeld and Nicolson, London, 2004. The first third of Richard David's one volume edition of *Hakluyt's Voyages* contains numerous descriptions of Arab enslavement of European seamen but little or nothing about European slavery see Richard David, Editor, *Hakluyt's Voyages*, Chatto and Windus, London, 1981.
31. For analysis of the validity of personal feelings of victimisation see Alyson M. Cole, *The Cult of True Victimhood: From the War of Welfare to the War on Terror*, Stanford University Press, Stanford, 2007.

CHAPTER 3

# From Heroes to Victims

**Abstract** Dramatic changes in attitudes towards warfare occurred in much of the West after the First World War, but these were caused by wider factors than the war itself. These included the spread of education, the development of the media and the reduction in the size of families. Subsequently reporting on wars has changed from lauding the heroes and the successful generals to lamenting the deaths and destruction. Each development in communications technology and particularly television has made the suffering more visible to an ever wider public while any differentiation there was in past wars between civilians and soldiers has often been removed by technical and political changes. Given the spread of knowledge about the effects of warfare the most popular nations worldwide are those that appear peaceful and constructive.

**Keywords** 1914–1918 • Heroes • Media • Monuments • Mourning

For centuries powerful nations boasted of their victories in historic battles. They raised triumphal arches, built statues and named streets, squares and even cities after their successful soldiers and sailors to keep the memories of victories alive. The history they wrote and taught was largely about such battles. Nations were the predominant historical actors and they were involved in an intermittent struggle in which only the strongest would survive and prosper. Weaker nations looked back to times when they were not repressed by aggressive empires and when they too had been amongst the strong. But mass politics and increased travel and communication have produced a revolution. The victimised now have more influence and even victorious nations have found it convenient both for domestic and international reasons to stress their past sufferings.

Many would argue that it was the First World War that brought this revolution. The carnage in the trenches was so great and the effects were so destabilising that the victors had little over which to rejoice when the fighting stopped in November 1918. As one of the leading experts in the field, Jay Winter of Yale University, has suggested, 'the bloodshed had reached a level never seen before' and there was 'suffering on a scale never before known'.[1] This is indeed how that war is generally regarded but the proportion of Britons killed in the First World War was approximately the same as the proportion who died in the French wars a century earlier. However, they were killed over a much shorter time and in a different way; the First World War lasted for 4 years as against 23 years of intermittent combat against France. Moreover, as two analysts of previous conflicts pointed out, '125,000 out of 185,000 (73 %) sailors recruited for the Seven Years War (1756–1763) died of disease … Scarcely one in ten of those embarked returned from the failed expedition to Cartagena … 23,000 died of disease, compared with 217 killed in action in the expedition to the Dutch island of Walcheren in 1809.'[2]

In other words, earlier campaigns could be more lethal but in the First World War fewer died of sickness and more through shell and rifle fire and poisonous gases. People were accustomed to death from illness, as shown by their relatively calm reaction to the influenza pandemic which followed the war and carried off tens of thousands in Britain and millions worldwide. But people were not used to violence on an epochal scale and it was the violence of the Western Front which was so shocking. There is some parallel today to the Western reaction to terrorism where, 9/11 apart, terrorists have so far managed to kill only a fraction of those who die in traffic accidents in the West but far more attention is devoted to terrorist attacks because they are unexpected, sudden and gratuitous. Wars remain particularly shocking though the World Health Organisation believes that suicide sometimes causes more than twice as many deaths across the world (815,000 in 2000 against 310,000).[3]

Finally, and most importantly, the First World War's impact was all the greater because it interacted with the underlying changes in society. Mass education, the expansion of the franchise and the spread of popular newspapers meant that soldiers from a poor background mattered in 1914 as they had not done in previous great wars. Unlike most of their illiterate ancestors, people *knew* something of what was happening on the battlefields and could imagine the fate of their relatives. Further, with much smaller families and a lower birth rate than people had during the French wars, they felt each loss more deeply than their predecessors had done. Accordingly, for the first time each village church mourned the dead with a plaque recording their names while acres of French countryside were covered with the graves of those who had been killed in the fighting. They are now much more carefully tended by the Commonwealth War Graves Commission established in 1917 than their civilian counterparts in the average churchyard in Britain.

Some have said that the failure to find or identify all the bodies of the fallen increased the sufferings of their families compared with earlier wars but there were far fewer records kept of the burial places of ordinary soldiers and sailors in the past. For the most part, as far as their families were concerned, they just went away and never came back.[4] Yet mourning seems to have been less in the nineteenth century and before, once again one comes back to the reduction in family size, the acknowledgement that everyone who fell should be remembered, the way soldiers died and the greater knowledge of what happened on the battlefields to explain the reaction. Every major change in communications over the past 200 years has produced a corresponding change in political culture.

Soldiers were widely regarded as the main victims of the First World War. In contrast, in the Second World War and afterwards it was civilians who were increasingly seen as the victims of conflict and armed forces as the potential victimisers. The deliberate massacre of civilians on the Eastern Front and in Asia, the Holocaust, the naval blockades and the strategic bombing campaigns all meant that civilians were 'in the firing line' as much as the soldiers and sailors. The subsequent guerrilla campaigns against the colonial powers from Kenya to Malaya and Vietnam to Algeria further blurred the distinction between military forces and civilians.

The successive development of radio, film and particularly television meant that civilians across much of the world had an ever more vivid idea of the destruction wrought by conflict. Journalists talk nowadays about the media's fascination with war but equally important is the way in which the focus and tone of their reports has changed.[5] Until the end of the nineteenth century battles could still be reported in terms of the strategic skill of the commanders and the bravery of the soldiers involved particularly if the people writing about them were nationals of one of the combatants. Thus a later British description of the battle of Waterloo in 1815 might be larded with some two dozen references to the 'gallantry' of both sides, a British description of the siege of Sedan between the Prussians and the French in 1870 might have half as many.[6] The most famous of the British war correspondents, W. H. Russell of *The Times* described individual battles in great detail rather as a football match might be described today on the radio and with spectators shouting their enthusiasm at great examples of bravery. Nevertheless, he also described the horrors, the dead packed into graves, the wounded lying for days on the battlefield and the looting of their clothes and boots.[7] The names of British admirals and generals were widely known amongst the general public. Before photography became pervasive, artists drew the contorted faces of the people involved in hand-to-hand combat to emphasise the points made in the text and to personalise battles.

In contrast, in modern warfare the servicemen and women involved have been enveloped by the tanks, ships or aircraft which they control. Journalists rarely describe the fighting itself in any detail and adjectives are largely reserved for the impact of battles on the civilians living in the area. There were some references in nineteenth-century literature to such victims depending on the reporter but they were generally rarer. In his description of the siege of Sedan during the Franco-Prussian War Charles Lowe, *The Times*' correspondent in Berlin devoted one sentence to the 'women, children and wounded' killed in 1870 by Prussian artillery and to the 'shrieks, curses and groans' of the wounded though he did mention the French Emperor's horror at the devastation and his efforts to broker peace.[8] On the other hand, Edward Dicey who covered the Austro-Prussian War against Denmark in 1864 and the Prussian conflict with Austria 2 years later for the *Daily Telegraph* put a good deal of stress on the flight of civilians from the towns and their suffering as the German forces advanced.[9] By the end of the century governments that appeared to be mistreating civilians were fiercely criticised at home and abroad and some felt obliged to respond. The rounding up by British troops of Boer women and children and the systematic destruction of their farms during the Boer War was so unpopular in Britain itself that, after the end of the fighting, the victorious British paid to restock and rebuild the farms and to provide other forms of compensation.[10]

At the start of the nineteenth-century war was widely romanticized not least because the educated were soaked in the classical literature of Homer and Caesar for whom war was the supreme test for man and country. But the less educated shared many of the same feelings. Just as Shakespeare imagined Henry V appealing to his soldiers before the Battle of Agincourt in 1415 so Napoleon encouraged his troops before combat by reminding them of the 'glory' in which they were about to share. An officer who heard his speech before the battle of Borodino during the French invasion of Russia in 1812 commented 'who is there that would not have rushed forward, replete with joy and hope, and disdaining an odious and disgraceful repose'.[11] He stressed the way in which the Russian armies had laid their own country waste to hinder the French advance but, typically for a soldier of the time, he gave little space in his memoirs to the impact on civilians who must have starved or frozen to death in their thousands.

Nineteenth-century poets from the long-time Poet Laureate, Alfred Lord Tennyson to the Nobel Prize winning poet, Rudyard Kipling found soldiers and war more interesting and relevant to their readers than their successors would do in the twenty-first century. Tennyson's poems reflected the tension between romanticising the courage shown in such futile but heroic wartime actions as 'the charge of the Light Brigade' in the Crimea on the one hand and deploring the destruction war brought on the other. But the suffering became more prominent in his work as the years went by. 'Locksley Hall' one of the poems which Tennyson published in 1842 was more optimistic than 'Locksley Hall Sixty Years After' which he wrote in old age and published in 1887. In one of the most famous and prescient lines in the English language the earlier poem envisaged 'aircraft' carrying precious goods around the world but also dropping chemical weapons until, presumably as a reaction, the 'Parliament of Man' was established when the battle-flags would be furled and conflict would cease.[12]

Descriptions of the battles for cities in Iraq and Syria during the civil wars in those countries at the beginning of the twenty-first century focus almost entirely on the fate of the civilian population. There might be fleeting references to the commanders of the armies involved and to the 'house-to-house' fighting but comments on the 'glory' of war would be unimaginable as generally would the idea of emphasising the bravery of the individual combatants particularly on the 'other' side. The heroes are the medical staff who risk their lives to help the sick and wounded or the representatives of the UN and non-governmental agencies who struggle to bring food to the starving. It is they who are interviewed and explain the situation and their own problems. The Islamist suicide bombers and their like are portrayed as deranged or drugged not brave or gallant precisely because they set out to 'give their lives' in combat. Photographic coverage shows the destruction of buildings within a city and the refugees fleeing for their lives. This dramatic change in media perspective parallels the emphasis given by the modern media to disaster, controversy and threats rather than success, agreement and progress. The negotiation of a successful agreement limiting the production or use of weaponry is largely ignored and wars that are apparently ended by peacekeeping missions disappear from the news.[13]

The general change in the perspective on warfare and military power has an impact on Western armed forces though not perhaps as much as one might expect.[14] Partly because of the cost and the increasing technicality of modern warfare most Western countries have now abandoned conscription and rely on smaller, professional armed services that continue to attract capable volunteers. These want their courage and potential sacrifices to be appreciated but to avoid being seen as pitiful victims any more than racing drivers, mountain climbers or explorers want to be seen as victims if they are killed in the course of their vocation. Those who join the armed forces know that they are possibly going to have to risk their lives in a war not of their own choosing.[15] This is true not only of the servicemen but also of the women who have demanded the right to serve in virtually every role in the armed forces and to take part in battles—it is a very far cry from the World Wars where armed forces tried to keep women as far away as possible from the various fronts.

During conflicts in which their forces are involved Western governments are under increasing pressure to apologise for actions that are considered to have led to 'unnecessary' or accidental loss of life. Thus, US Secretary of State, Madeline Albright apologised to the Chinese Ambassador after US forces bombed the Chinese Embassy in Belgrade in May 1999 during the campaign to coerce the Serb forces to leave Kosovo. In the middle of the night Albright and the Vice Chairman of the Joint Chiefs, General Joseph Ralston went to the Chinese Embassy in Washington and apologised to the Ambassador both in private and on Chinese television.[16] This was a remarkable, probably unique, action for such a senior representative of a great power. The US subsequently paid compensation. In October 2015 President Obama later apologised to the Afghan President and to the International President of Medecins Sans Frontieres, when an Afghan hospital run by that charity was bombed by US forces. The United

States apologised again after its aircraft unintentionally attacked Syrian government forces in September 2016 killing 62 soldiers.[17]

Walk down Whitehall in the centre of London and you see reflections of the change in attitudes. Outside the Ministry of Defence and opposite the Foreign and Commonwealth Office are the statues of successful generals, a mile away on the other side of the Thames is Waterloo Station and nearby is Trafalgar Square and Nelson's column commemorating successes during the Napoleonic Wars. But there are few ceremonies surrounding these reminders of past victories and many of those who pass by have little or nothing about such events lodged in their memories.[18] Although he gave his name to one of the most important squares in London, many would today be hard put to remember who Nelson was. One survey published in October 2017 found that a third of those replying did not know that France and the US were on the British side in the Second World War and one in 20 believed Britain was on the same side as Germany, Italy and Japan. One in 10 admitted they did not know Hitler was involved in the War.[19]

If ignorance of more recent events was so great, ignorance of Admiral Nelson was likely to be even greater though he was the most popular British hero of the Napoleonic Wars. Within a decade of his death at the battle of Trafalgar in 1805 the Poet Laureate Robert Southey wrote in his *Life of Nelson* 'he cannot be said to have fallen prematurely whose work was done; nor ought he to be lamented who died so full of honours, and at the height of human fame. The most splendid [death is] that of the hero in the hour of victory'.[20] Such language underlines the very different attitude towards military prowess prevalent at the time.

Instead of tributes to victories, each November the nation's leaders gather near the Cenotaph in the middle of Whitehall to mourn those who died during the First World War and later conflicts. Half a mile away in Westminster Abbey there is the tomb where the 'unknown warrior' from the First World War was buried in 1920. He may not have been a 'warrior', he might have been a poor soldier, unable to keep in step and the butt of complaints from officers and fellows. But it is not his unknown achievements that are lamented; it is his status as one of the hundreds of thousands of volunteers and conscripted soldiers who were victims of the fighting. The ceremonies at the Cenotaph are replicated on a smaller scale across the country and they have continued to be observed as the decades have passed.

The generals and admirals are little remembered while sportsmen, popular singers and the ersatz heroes of the screen are recalled. Nineteenth-century British railway stations were named after military victories, but airports, which are their twentieth- and twenty-first-century equivalents, are named after unfortunate 'celebrities' who died relatively young. Liverpool airport was renamed after the singer, John Lennon and Belfast City after the footballer, George Best. What they have in common apart from their fame and the pleasure they gave to those who watched or listened to them is that they were both victims; Best of his alcoholism and Lennon of an assassin. Similarly, in the United States Idlewild Airport near New York was renamed in December 1963 after President John Kennedy following his murder. Kennedy was different from Lennon and Best because he had held power but it was not primarily for his success as a statesman that he was commemorated, even though he saved the developed countries from the utter disaster of a nuclear war during the Cuba missile crisis in 1962. It was his sudden death at an early age which shocked people across the world. Similarly, in Britain Princess Diana's death in 1997 in a traffic accident caused an outpouring of grief because of her youth and beauty. This is the time of what used to be called the 'common people' and they often see themselves as pushed around or betrayed by politicians, generals, bankers and industrialists. He or she is the victim of history and they identify themselves with popular and well-liked victims. Conspiracy theories now counter the official explanations for dramatic events and make famous people who die suddenly the alleged victims of government plots.[21]

The reaction to Diana's death in a car accident in Paris in 1997 was as typical of the time as the reaction to Nelson's death was in 1805. Diana was a victim and as the Prime Minister, Tony Blair said at the time, she was the 'People's Princess' in other words she was the heroine of the mass of people rather than just the elite. She was seen as the victim because her husband, the heir to the throne, Prince Charles was believed to have never really loved her, continued an affair with another woman after his marriage and eventually divorced her. She was also seen as the victim of the very media that made her famous and of the British Royal Family who some believed ostracised her, particularly after her estrangement from Charles. So much were these groups seen as the victimisers that, immediately after her death, rumours grew that she had been assassinated by the agents of the Royal Family. There were also more realistic suggestions that it was the media who were responsible for her death by the way in which the photographers had been chasing her car. This was overloaded with armour and was travelling at high speed to escape them through a tunnel with a low speed limit. Official investigations both in France and Britain found no evidence of a conspiracy against Diana instead they showed that the driver was taking anti-depressants and had been drinking alcohol during the course of the evening.

There are memorials in many parts of the world to the hapless Jews murdered in the Holocaust. The sufferings of the native peoples killed, infected with disease or thrust aside by the European settlers in Canada, the United States, New Zealand and Australia are for the first time given prominence. Hollywood's films used to portray American settlers heroically defending themselves in their wagons against the depredations of the 'Red Indians' who were inexplicably attacking them with their bows and arrows. Now, films reflect the horrors of the slave trade, the Holocaust and the mistreatment of allied prisoners during the Second World War. Popular television programmes trace the ancestry of television presenters, sportsmen and women; such ancestors generally turn out to be victims of the workhouse or even of slavery rather than the aristocrats who lorded it over the majority of the population.

This reflects a wider and much more sensitive view of history than that held in the past. Calm discussions of the way in which one's own nation or group has caused suffering to others peoples can sometimes help heal rifts between peoples. But excessive and emotional focus on the way in which other nations have damaged our own can be as threatening as the boasts that strong nations used to voice about their victories. It can cause loathing between peoples and it is often used by unsatisfied governments which want to mobilise their countrymen to change the status quo or to divert their attention from their own past failings. Bitter feelings about the past are currently used by those with influence or power across East Asia and the Middle East to encourage hostility towards neighbouring states or other religions. Violent emotions can simmer under the surface of pleas of past suffering.

In the absence of memories of victimisation, most people fear or dislike the use of military power by foreigners sometimes even when they believe that the objectives sought may be beneficial. With the development of world-wide opinion polls we can see for the first time how, at any threat of such activity, the popularity of a state rapidly declines amongst other nations. The most favoured countries are stable, prosperous, democratic and cautious with the use of their armed forces. In 2014 Germany and Canada were rated the most positively in a survey by the BBC World Service and Britain was the third most popular.[22] In contrast, Japan, which had been the most favourably ranked country in 2012, had been caught in wrangles with China over claims to islands in the East China Sea and intensified arguments about history with both China and South Korea. Most South Koreans and Chinese now regarded Japan negatively. China's growing economic power had sometimes been welcomed in earlier years but its confrontational posture with Japan and also with the states bordering the South China Sea had taken their toll. In 2011, according to Pew, majorities in much of Western Europe believed that its growing military power was a 'bad thing' for their country.[23]

In 2003 most Europeans also objected to the US taking action to depose the Iraqi dictator, Saddam Hussein and, after the attack took place, majorities in such long-term allies of the US as South Korea and Turkey were so alienated that they professed disappointment at Iraq's lack of resistance.[24] Yet most in Western Europe, though not in Russia or Turkey, thought the Iraqi people would be better off without the dictator with less than 20 % in Britain, France, Germany and Italy arguing the reverse.[25] Majorities also believed that the Middle East would be more stable. In other words, even to achieve what they thought was desirable, the use of military power was wrong or likely to be ineffective. The majority felt that US foreign policy had a negative effect on their country though in Western Europe this was predominantly seen as peculiar to the Bush administration rather than the US in general.[26]

Once Barak Obama took office in 2009, this swung dramatically, though not universally, with over 90 % of Germans and French expressing confidence in his leadership.[27] Presumably this was in part because he seemed likely to follow a more cautious foreign policy. There was a subsequent decline in the 'Obama Bounce' because some of the administration's previous supporters felt that its achievements were disappointing. Its widespread use of drones against Islamists in Pakistan and Yemen provoked hostility in the Islamic world even if terrorism and religious extremism were widely feared in such countries.[28] On the other hand, the 'Islamic State' in Iraq and Syria made itself so abhorrent and its threats were so ubiquitous that by 2015 the US air campaign against it was backed by most countries polled by Pew with Russia, Malaysia, Pakistan and Argentina as exceptions. Overall 62 % of those polled across the world supported US actions.[29]

Very often however the only people who do favour the use of military power and violence are nationals of the states initiating it (though by no means all of those) and sometimes allies or sympathisers with the initiators. Thus in 1980 over a third of Pakistanis supported the seizure of American embassy officials in Teheran as hostages in order to coerce Washington into handing over the former Shah of Iran who had fled into exile.[30] Similarly, when Israeli forces invaded Lebanon to attack Palestinian guerrillas over 40 % of Americans continued to favour Israel and only some 9 % backed the Palestinians.[31] In 2009 after Israel had bombarded the Gaza strip in response to missile attacks, the majority of Americans continued to blame the Palestinians for the violence but a third criticised Israel's military response and nearly a quarter thought it had 'gone too far'.[32] Admittedly in the abstract, West European males are inclined to accept that it is sometimes necessary to use force to maintain international order and protect the victimised but three quarters of Germans and Spanish believe UN approval is necessary for this and substantial majorities in Britain and France.[33]

Some maintain that such attitudes distinguish Western Europe from the United States. In 2003 the American analyst, Robert Kagan argued that 'on major strategic and international issues today, Americans are from Mars and Europeans are from Venus. They agree on little and understand one another less and less.'[34] This was at least an exaggeration or simplification. Traditionally Americans were more cautious than Europeans about the use of military power; at the peak of isolationist feeling in 1937 over 60 % lamented their country's entry into the First World War. In the 1970s only 26 % of the less educated and 38 % of the educated were in favour of sending troops to help a friendly state under attack and over 80 % wanted close cooperation with the Soviet Union to avoid war.[35] In 2014 only a quarter of Americans backed sending help to Taiwan if the island were attacked by China, sympathy for the potential victims of aggression could only go so far.[36]

Throughout the Cold War years Americans were more gloomy about the prospects of a world war than the Europeans; in 1982 and 1986 just under half the Americans polled said there was a 50 % chance of a world war breaking out in the next 10 years while the figures for Britain were 29 % in 1982 and 20 % in 1986 and for Italy 25 % and 22 %.[37] Such contrasts do not obviously suggest that US opinion was particularly 'Martian'.

Powerful states can dismiss international opinion because others need to trade and have diplomatic relations with them however they behave.

Indeed, weak states may be cowed into appeasing them if they appear aggressive. But there are disadvantages to being unpopular because it constrains diplomatic options and, in extreme cases, will encourage states to form hostile blocs.[38] The invasion of Iraq in 2003 turned the Iraqis into victims for many who watched its progress on television.[39] This meant that Germany, France and other allies refused to cooperate and that the governments in states, such as Britain, which did send forces to assist the US attack, faced criticism from large sections of their own people and indeed from some of their own political supporters. Israelis are conscious of the hostility their country's uses of military force evoke but they still vote for governments which order them because their historical memories have taught them that they live in a world where only brute force ensures survival.[40] Naturally they stress their centuries of victimisation culminating in the horror of the Holocaust because victimisation now provides one of the few justifications for the use of force that have global credibility.

As the second part of this book will show, governments and opinion formers in satisfied countries, such as Britain and the United States, appeal to vicarious victimisation when they want to justify military actions. Critics often suggest that these justifications hide the 'real' reasons for their belligerence but it is more likely that they stress those which had most public appeal. The British government stressed the German invasion of the small state of Belgium in breach of international law when they went to war in August 1914. Undoubtedly, they were afraid that Germany might otherwise defeat France and Russia and then go on to threaten Britain. But they were also angered by what they saw as German aggression and lawlessness. In other cases hidden motives were fairly weak. The Western nations used force against Serbia in the 1990s because they sympathised with the Bosniaks and with the Muslim inhabitants of Kosovo over what they saw as their mistreatment at Serb hands. The Blair government sent forces to Sierra Leone because the stories of massacres were so horrific and perhaps because it had been Britain's first African colony and there was still some feeling of responsibility for what was happening.

What British and American governments have not done in the past is to focus on the historical victimisation of their own people even though they could have stigmatised foreign oppressors if they had chosen to do so. The exception is Donald Trump who successfully appealed to US self-pity during the 2016 election campaign. But there were many other possibilities; after the fall of Singapore and the Philippines in 1942, the Japanese tortured, starved and worked to death thousands of British and American prisoners of war. The survivors have written dozens of accounts of their suffering, there have also been films as well as television and radio programmes in plenty of the episode. Yet there has never been a government-sponsored mass campaign for apologies or compensation like the Korean, Chinese, Filipino and Taiwanese campaigns for apologies for the women forced to prostitute themselves to the Japanese army during the Second World War or the Chinese campaign for apologies from Japan for the killing of uncountable thousands of Chinese civilians in Nanjing and elsewhere.

Governments in London and Washington have generally taken a pragmatic view of such issues and were concerned with trade and contemporary relations not with historic crimes. More focused on economic advantage and making the best of the present than the Marxist government in Beijing, they were happy with the system which they established. Government behaviour both reflected and encouraged the British and American public also to take a pragmatic attitude towards other nations. The results were reflected in Pew's April 2015 poll where almost equal number of Americans and Japanese either said that Japan had apologised sufficiently for the Second World War or that no apology was necessary (61 % and 63 % respectively).[41]

At one time, elites tended to believe that the mass of people were vindictive, emotional and untrustworthy. Experience has shown that this is not the case in Britain. In November and December 1940 after the German bombing raids on London, Coventry and other cities, opinion was evenly divided on whether or not it favoured bombing German civilians in retaliation and on whether the enemy was only the Nazi government or the German people as a whole.[42] Towards the end of the war 44 % wanted to see Germany controlled and disarmed against 26 % who wanted it crippled or divided into separate states.[43] At the same time, over 70 % approved the decision to drop atomic bombs on Japan but that, no doubt, reflected relief that the conflict was finally over and impatience with the Japanese for prolonging the suffering when they were clearly beaten. A warrior people might have admired the enemy's courage, an unmilitary public just thought they were wasting lives to no good effect. In any case, it was not the mob or elderly baying for blood who backed the use of nuclear weapons, those on higher incomes and those in their twenties were slightly more favourable to their use than the poorer and older.[44]

Politicians only gradually accepted what the polls told them about public opinion. But, when they did, they began to realise that the majority of their fellow citizens were not, or no longer, untrustworthy and irresponsible, they were only too well aware of the implications of the threats to their fate. Britain was supposed to be deeply divided by class and education but polls generally showed this to be mistaken as far as most foreign issues were concerned. The vote to leave the European Union in 2016 was one of the occasions when the opposite was to some extent the case.

Just as the politicians realised the mass of people were not the fools that they had sometimes taken them to be so the electorate discovered that their own judgement was often as good, and sometimes better, than the politicians'. The crude opinion polls available suggest that they saw before Neville Chamberlain admitted it that the Nazis could not be appeased.[45] They felt that Anthony Eden's attempt to recapture the Suez Canal after the Egyptians nationalised it in 1956 was a mistake and similarly knew in 2001 that British involvement in US operations in Afghanistan would increase rather than reduce the terrorist threat to Britain despite government claims that the reverse was true.[46] The public also saw that governments often did not know how to improve the state of the economy and that they and the economists were guessing what to do.

Unfortunately, though unsurprisingly, this has encouraged widespread unease with the political elite whereas the last part of this book will show that governmental mistakes are often a result of the inherent difficulties of interpreting the past and thus forecasting the future. Governments have to feel their way towards solutions to problems and now they have to do so under intense media and public scrutiny. This has been very much the case with the response by politicians in the complacent powers to protests from the dissatisfied nations and groups that are analysed later in this book.

## Notes

1. Jay Winter, Editor, *The Legacy of the Great War: Ninety Years on*, University of Missouri Press, Columbia, 2009, pp. 74 and 84.
2. David Coleman and John Salt, *Patterns, Trends, and Processes*, Oxford University Press, Oxford, 1992, p. 24. See also the provocative Hans Zinsser, *Rats, Lice and History*, Bantam, New York, 1965. pp. 111–122.
3. 'Suicide lead cause of international deaths', *Los Angeles Times*, 4 October 2002.
4. For the opposite point of view see Pat Jalland, *Death in War and Peace: Loss and Grief in England, 1914–1970*, Oxford University Press, Oxford, 2010, chapter 3.

5. Kate Adie, 'The media portrayal of the military' in Stephen Badsey, Editor, *The Media and International Security*, Frank Cass, London, 2000, pp. 51–63.
6. Archibald Forbes et al., *Battles of the Nineteenth Century*, Cassel, London, 1901, Volume 1, pp. 54–70.
7. Elizabeth Grey, *The Noise of Drums and Trumpets: W. H. Russell's Reports from Crimea*, Longmans, London, 1971, pp. 115, 116, 128, 131 and 139.
8. Forbes, *Battles*, Volume 11, p. 98.
9. Edward Dicey, *The Schleswig-Holstein War*, Tinsley Brothers, London, 1864, Volume 1, p. 264. See also Dicey's comments on the later war in Edward Dicey, *The Battle-Fields of 1866*, Tinsley Brothers, London, 1866, pp. 132–133.
10. G. B. Beak, *The Aftermath of War: An Account of the Repatriation of Boers and Natives in the Orange River Colony 1902–1904*, Edward Arnold, London, 1906.
11. General Count Philippe de Ségur, *History of the Expedition to Russia, 1812*, Stroud, 2005, Volume 1, p. 92.
12. 'Locksley Hall' and 'Locksley Hall Sixty Years After' in *The Works of Alfred Lord Tennyson*, Macmillan, London, 1893, pp. 101 and 564.
13. Philip Towle, 'The media, megaphone diplomacy and disarmament' in Badsey, *Media and International Security*, pp. 227–236.
14. For discussion of the relationship between journalists and the military see Peter Young and Peter Jesser, *The Media and the Military*, Macmillan, Basingstoke, 1977; Michael Herr, *Dispatches*, Alfred A. Knopf, New York, 1977, pp. 189–195; Max Hastings, *Going to the Wars*, Macmillan, Basingstoke, 2000, pp. xi–xvi.
15. They may indeed strongly oppose the particular wars in which they are involved see Hugh Tinker, *A Message from the Falklands*, Junction Books, London, 1982.
16. Madeleine Albright, *Madam Secretary: A Memoir*, Macmillan, London, 2003, p. 417.
17. 'The Ceasefire unravels', *The Economist*, 24 September 2016, p. 51.
18. See the eulogy of 'our great national hero' by Robert Southey, *Life of Nelson*, first published 1813, new edition Hutchinson, London, 1905, preface.
19. 'Adolf Hitler: What did he have to do with the War?' *Daily Telegraph*, 9 October 2017.
20. Southey, *Nelson*, p. 338. For a modern assessment see Roger Knight, *The Pursuit of Victory: The Life and Achievement of Horatio Nelson*, Penguin, London, 2005, p. 558.
21. Daniel Pipes, *Conspiracy*, Free Press, New York, 1999; David Ray Griffin, *The 9/11 Commission Report: Omissions and Distortions*, Arris Books,

Moreton-in-Marsh, 2005; Vian Bakir and David M. Barlow Editors, *Communication in the Age of Suspicion: Trust and the Media*, Palgrave, Basingstoke, 2007. 'They lied about May Lai. And I tell you they lied about bin Laden', *Sunday Times*, 24 April, 2016.

22. BBC World Service Poll by GlobeScan, 'Presentation of Results on Ratings of Different Countries', 4 July 2014, compiled by Gallup Pakistan.
23. 'China seen overtaking US as global superpower', Pew Research Center, 13 July 2011.
24. 'Views of a Changing World 2003', Pew Research Center, 3 June 2003, p. 3.
25. 'America's image further erodes; Europe wants weaker ties', Pew Research Center, 18 March 2003, p. 4.
26. 'America's image further erodes, Europe wants weaker ties', Pew Research Center, 18 March 2003.
27. 'From hyperpower to declining power', Pew Global Attitudes Project, 7 September 2011, p. 3.
28. For an analysis of this type of warfare see Chris Woods, *Sudden Justice: America's Secret Drone Wars*, Hurst, London, 2015. 'Islamic extremism causes concern for Muslims and Western countries', Pew Global Attitudes Project, 14 July 2005.
29. 'Global publics back US on fighting ISIS but are critical of post 9/11 torture', Pew Research Center, 23 June 2015.
30. 'Public opinion in Pakistan in the year 1980', Gilani Research Foundation, 2 September 2014.
31. 'American' support for Israel unchanged by recent hostilities', Pew Research Center, 26 July 2006.
32. 'Modest backing for Israel in Gaza crisis', Pew Research Center, 13 January 2013.
33. 'The American-Western European values gap', Pew Research Center, 17 November 2011. See Robert Kagan, *Of Paradise and Power: America and Europe in the New World Order*, Knopf, New York, 2003.
34. Kagan, *Paradise*, p. 3.
35. Robert Oldendick and Barbara Bordes, 'Mass and Elite Foreign Policy Opinion', *Public Opinion Quarterly*, February 1982, p. 374; See also Hazel Erskine, 'The polls: is war a mistake?' *Public Opinion Quarterly*, 1970–1971, p. 135.
36. 'Americans neutral on Taiwan', *Taipei Times*, 18 September 2014.
37. Tom W. Smith, 'The polls—A Report: Nuclear Anxiety', *Public Opinion Quarterly*, Winter 1988, p. 563.
38. For a classic defence of the balance of power see Max Beloff, *The Balance of Power*, George Allen and Unwin, London, 1968. For alliances forming in response to Chinese expansionism see 'China v the rest', *The Economist*, 26 March 2016, p. 63.

39. See 'How children in Germany perceived the war in Iraq' in Defra Lemish and Maya Gotz Editors, *Children and the Media in Times of War and Conflict*, Hampton Press, Creskill, New Jersey, 2007, pp. 17–33. See also p. 92 on Dutch children's reactions.
40. In the BBC World Service poll for 2014 Israel was one of the four most unpopular countries alongside North Korea, Iran and Pakistan.
41. 'Americans, Japanese mutual respect 70 years after the end of World War II', Pew Research Center, 7 April 2015.
42. 'Gallup and Fortune Polls: British Reactions', *Public Opinion Quarterly*, 1941, p. 157.
43. 'In Britain', *Public Opinion Quarterly*, 1944, p. 294.
44. Hadley Cantril and Mildred Strunk, *Public Opinion 1935–1946*, Princeton University Press, Princeton, 1951, p. 20.
45. See the crude opinion polls in 'British Institute of Public Opinion', Public Opinion Quarterly, 1940, pp. 77–80.
46. Jean Owen, 'The public and newspaper appraisals of the Suez Crisis' and 'Gallup Opinion Polls', *Public Opinion Quarterly*, 1957–1958, pp. 350–354, 383–384, 391 and 395. 'War on Afghanistan', poll 11 October 2001, Granada, p. 2. See also the later poll '72 per cent of Britons expecting terror attack', *The Times*, 7 April 2004.

CHAPTER 4

# A Gratitude Free Zone

**Abstract** Gratitude is much rarer in politics than complaints, anger and resentment. Personal contacts sometimes help to reduce hatreds as after the Second World War when the occupying forces often came to sympathise with their defeated and starving enemies. But personal ties can be broken by tides of fanaticism as happened in the Cultural Revolution in China and close relations between one government and another are not carried over to the next. Colonial forces abandon those who have helped them and countries rarely admit that they are grateful to other nations because people find such admissions demeaning. Thus, although gratitude is constructive and builds confidence, resentment is more pervasive.

**Keywords** Colonialism • Depersonalisation • Empathy • Forgetfulness • Meetings

The political effectiveness of complaints about past suffering is best illustrated by contrasting them with their opposite, that is gratitude or understanding. International affairs are largely a gratitude free zone yet gratitude and understanding are constructive rather than destructive because they evoke reciprocal good feeling. One might also expect them to shape habits and conventions so that, even if the incidents which gave rise to them were not fixed in the conscious memory, they would continue to be

© The Author(s) 2018
P. Towle, *History, Empathy and Conflict*,
https://doi.org/10.1007/978-3-319-77959-1_4

effective. Unfortunately anger, hatred and the desire for revenge for past and present suffering are much easier to stir in mass audiences and more powerful. Foreigners can be depersonalised or caricatured. The mistakes or crimes committed in the past by a few can be represented as general characteristics.

By contrast to mass opinion formed by such political speeches, personal contacts may sometimes lead to positive emotions such as empathy for their suffering. At the end of the Second World War the invading troops gradually discovered that most of their former enemies in Germany and Japan were pitiable humans struggling to survive after the collapse of their governments and economies. Colonel Byford-Jones recalled later that in Berlin 'there were no medical supplies, not even anaesthetics, heart stimulants or sulphonamides. Food was poor and at starvation level, and nutrition was bad. The death-rate was high and continued to be high. There was a vast and uncontrolled movement of epidemic disease-carrying refugees from the East, who were living in ruins, in cellars and places with no sanitation'.[1] In such circumstances the anger which had built up against the German people gradually melted away and they came to seem the victims. Another member of the British occupation forces, Noel Annan commented, 'our troops who at first considered the Germans were getting their just deserts became ever more sympathetic to them and hostile to the d[isplaced] p[ersons] when they had to turn out night after night to stop some affray' between Germans and former foreign slaves or 'guest workers' who were wandering round the country and taking revenge on the 'master race'.[2]

Those bent on revenge for past victimisation have sometimes drawn back when they met face to face with the people they were planning to attack. Laura Blumenfeld, a young Jewish American tracked down the family of the Palestinian who shot her father but discovered how sympathetic they were as a group and how generous and friendly despite their hardships.[3] They were as much victims of circumstance as her father. Terrorists have occasionally begun to doubt the wisdom of their cause when faced with their potential victims. Eamon Collins, an IRA activist, found that Major Ivan Toombs, the first man he was asked to help assassinate, was a kind, rather impressive person. Eventually Collins broke with the IRA and was murdered in front of his house for his disloyalty and his determination to talk and write about his experience.[4]

Unfortunately, pressure from those in power and mob feelings can sometimes break down personal links however strong. Two of the accounts by former Red Guards show how this process worked during the Cultural Revolution in China in the 1960s. Mao's government had polarised China by starting the so-called 'Hundred Flowers Movement' in which everyone was encouraged to voice their opinions even if they were critical of current policies. Many had taken the opportunity offered. The universities were divided between those who wanted to focus on academic work and those closer to Mao's views who wanted to spend time labouring with workers and peasants. During the subsequent Cultural Revolution the government encouraged the students to turn on the critics and those who had stressed academic learning.[5] Dai Hsiao-ai recalled later that he was initially both surprised and reluctant; 'I was particularly close to the literature teacher and had always thought she was a good person and an excellent teacher. At first I was unwilling to criticise or struggle against her, but my classmates accused me of being sentimental ... The party could not be wrong'. After two weeks of persecution the unfortunate teacher showed signs of wanting to kill herself so the students put notices on her bed saying that they were watching her and would prevent her doing so.[6] The students 'forced the teachers to wear caps and collars which stated things like "I am a monster". Each class confronted and reviled them in turn with slogans, accusation and injunctions to reform their ways. We made them clean out the toilets, smeared them with black paint. They had little rest and were forced to sleep apart from their fellow teachers'. In Ken Ling's case he admitted that the persecution went far further. When the campaign against the teachers began, 'beatings and torture followed. I had never seen such torture before: eating nightsoil and insects; being subjected to electric shocks; forced to kneel on broken glass; being hanged "airplane" by arms and legs'. Many of the worst torturers were those who had done badly in their work. Lin's favourite teacher was tortured to death and his physics teacher committed suicide by jumping out of a window.[7]

The clash between empathy for current suffering and depersonalisation for previous alleged crimes or misbehaviour is visible even in the high politics of international relations. Here past friendships often fail to cement ties because statesmen believe they have to put their country's current interests before past debts. Today's friend may be tomorrow's enemy. After the end of the Second World War the Soviets and their former American and British allies against the Nazis spent more than three decades glowering at each other in the Cold War. Feelings of victimisation for past events are perpetuated while gratitude or thanks for past kindness or help, if it is felt at all, evaporates as memory fades. There are, of course, exceptions such as the Statue of Liberty which was paid for by private subscriptions raised in France in the 1870s and which celebrated the close relationship between the United States and France dating back to their cooperation during the American War of Independence in the eighteenth century. Similarly, as pointed out at the beginning of this book, many Western countries have annual days of remembrance when they meditate on the sacrifices made by those who lost their lives defending their countries over the last century. Even then the foreign contribution to their struggle can be forgotten; very few British people remember that Malta was awarded the George Cross for its suffering from bombing and naval blockade while acting as a British base during the Second World War. Very few appreciate the multinational nature of Bill Slim's army which protected India and drove the Japanese out of Burma.

When European empires retreated they often abandoned groups of people who had compromised themselves in the eyes of their compatriots by helping the occupying power.[8] One of the first territories to gain statehood from Britain was Iraq whose army almost immediately massacred Christian Assyrians who had been employed by the British to maintain order. A British officer who was in the area at the time recorded 2 years later, 'the [Iraqi] Army Command was quite certain in its own mind that, in its decision to wipe out the Assyrians, it would, in the ultimate issue, be backed not only by Arab public opinion, but by the Baghdad government'.[9] A historian wrote subsequently, 'Whitehall watched in horror as a pursuit degenerated into a pogrom, concluding that the army had run amok. But the Iraqis were jubilant; the troops returned to Mosul to triumphant arches; in Baghdad they were greeted with flowers and perfumes, with singing and cheering'.[10] The majority were venting their anger over past suffering under the Ottomans and later humiliation by the British against the hapless minority. The Christians had lived in Iraq for centuries before the foundation of Islam but the destruction of their community was completed after the Anglo-American intervention in Iraq in 2003. Journalists recorded that 'two thirds have left, as their friends and family have been killed by extremists. They have ended up eking out impoverished lives in the northern Kurdish region, or in Syria, Jordan and Egypt.'[11] The Patriarch who headed the largest Christian community in the country told journalists in 2014, 'for the first time in in the history of Iraq, Mosul is now empty of Christians.'[12] By contrast, the British did try in the 1930s to find a new home for the Assyrians in British Guiana, Brazil and elsewhere but, in the end, such efforts came to nothing and they also abandoned many supporters in other countries to their fate as they gradually withdrew from empire after 1945. The Americans gave sanctuary to some Vietnamese who had fought on their side in the 1960s but many were forgotten when they left the country in 1975. Imperialists and interventionists come and go often impervious to the catastrophic effect of their actions on those who have helped them.

Governments routinely display ingratitude to foreign statesmen who have been helpful to their country in the past.[13] Because gratitude is a weak emotion, its claims can easily be ignored in comparison with law, morality or political convenience. Many foreign leaders will have victimised sections of their own people, yet this was overlooked by politicians when their help was needed only to be recalled later when the former leaders, in turn, became victims. The last Shah of Iran was a long-standing friend of the West but, when he fled into exile in 1979, he was not welcomed to the United States. Even after he became terminally ill with cancer, President Carter only reluctantly and briefly allowed him into the US for medical treatment. One of the paradoxes was, indeed, that the 'doves' like Carter and his Secretary of State, Cyrus Vance were most inhospitable to the Shah because they prioritised current political convenience. On the other hand, the 'hawks', such as Henry Kissinger and Zbigniew Brzezinski, kept their memories fresh and were keenest to show their appreciation for his past assistance. In Britain Prime Minister Thatcher was initially in favour of permitting the former monarch to live on the estate he owned in the country but was dissuaded by the Foreign Office which predicted that the Iranians would revenge themselves on the British Embassy in Teheran.[14]

Subsequently President Pinochet of Chile helped Britain during its war with Argentina over the Falkland Islands in 1982 but, when he was visiting London in 1998, he was accused of victimising his own people during his time in power. Although he received support from Lady Thatcher, who had been Prime Minister in 1982, he was arrested and held in Britain for 18 months before the courts decided he was unfit to defend himself and was allowed to return to his own country.[15] President Mubarak of Egypt gave the Prime Minister, John Major warm support during the Gulf War of 1991 but the British government showed little sympathy for him when he was overthrown and imprisoned during the Arab Spring.[16] In these cases the former leader could be accused of viciously repressing his countrymen when he was in power although this had been ignored by the

British and US governments in the needs of the moment. Those who were in power when help was offered previous may keep the memories alive but national gratitude is ephemeral.

When one country benefits another the recipients often either stress what they believe are the disadvantages to the benefactors' policy or suggest that they are only acting out of self-interest. Russians might well be ignorant of the billions of dollars the US, Europe and Japan have spent in their country since the collapse of communism making safe Soviet nuclear submarines, material and weapons.[17] But, if they did know, they would probably say this was in the interests of the donors because they were afraid of nuclear terrorism and accidents spreading radiation. This is true but it ignores the possibility of multiple motives. Finally, it makes such mutually beneficial programmes more difficult to fund from Western tax payers.

The conventional wisdom is that appeals to gratitude are naïve in international affairs and that to balance the harm that some other people have done to one's ancestors by referring to the good they have done on other occasions is immoral, tasteless and insensitive. In any case, many benefits are provided over a considerable period and people forget what the world was like before they began. This was the case with the success of the United States first in defending and then rebuilding Europe economically from 1945 until the end of the Cold War. President Karzai of Afghanistan caused a shock in October 2013 when he told the BBC that the 12 years during which NATO forces had been fighting to stabilise his country had caused the Afghans great suffering. Two months later he told an Indian audience that Western people had to realise that his citizens were as human as they were. He was, of course, right to imply that there had been very heavy Afghan casualties and that these had been given much less attention in the Western media than those suffered by NATO forces. But there was widespread feeling in the West that he had been ungrateful for the sacrifices made to help his country.[18]

Modern Britons do not expect former colonial peoples to thank them for the cities, ports and railways which their Victorian ancestors built in their territories in the nineteenth century or the constitutional and educational systems they established. Rather they expect them to resent imperialism and to recall its victims instead of balancing its advantages and disadvantages or judging what their country might look like if it had never been incorporated into a European empire. It is not a question of such nice balances but of the deep feeling that being dominated was shameful and undermined their dignity. When the Indian writer, Nirad Chaudhuri dedicated one of his books 'to the memory of the British Empire in India ... All that was good and living within us was made, shaped and quickened by the same British rule', he was lampooned as a reactionary snob by his countrymen.[19] In January 2015 the Mayor of Taipei, Ko Wen-je was also derided when he suggested that the 'longer the colonisation, the more advanced a place is'. Professor Wang Hsiao-po of Shih Hsin University in Taipei argued that Hong Kong's prosperity was due to China's isolation under communism and Singapore's to its location, rather than the length of British rule there.[20]

Attempts to reduce current frictions by reminding other states of previous political, military or economic assistance may simply evoke fury. During the Korean War, the US representative, Warren Austin spoke to the United Nations of the way in which US missionaries had founded hospitals and schools in China over the previous century and how one-eighth of all Chinese graduates had studied at institutions developed by American Protestant missions. The Chinese responded to this speech not, as the US representative hoped, by showing appreciation or, at least, reducing their hostility but by denying that the United States had helped China. Instead they expelled all remaining missionaries on the grounds that they were spying, preparing a US invasion and trying to alter Chinese culture.[21] The intensity of their hatred for the West was so great that the Chinese communists could not accept that anything the missionaries had ever done was beneficial. They wanted to remind their people that they have been through a century of humiliation and suffering not that the period had also brought them many benefits when it introduced them to the modern world.

The prevalence of resentment and the rarity of gratitude in politics are in some ways counter-intuitive because gratitude encourages a donor to give further help. But it is only when nationalism is declining in a major country or group of nations, or they are gravely threatened, that they are willing to admit their past and current dependence. A classic example is Western Europe after the Second World War where once great nations were only too pleased to receive financial aid from the United States to restore their ruined cities and industries. They also recognised their need for US military assistance through NATO to keep the Soviets at bay and to prevent the resurgence of the local nationalism which had caused three wars over the previous century. But, even in Europe, it has been difficult to keep such gratitude alive.

## Notes

1. W. Byford-Jones, *Berlin Twilight*, Hutchinson, London, undated, pp. 21–22. See also Ulrike Jordan, Editor, *Conditions of Surrender: Britons and Germans Witness the End of the Second World War*, Tauris, London, 1997; Patricia Meehan, *A Strange Enemy People: Germans under British Rule, 1945–1950*, Peter Owen, London, 2001, For German accounts of their suffering see Lali Horstmann, *Nothing for Tears*, Weidenfeld and Nicolson, London, 1999, first published 1953; Anonymous, *A Woman in Berlin: Diary 20 April 1945 to 22 June 1945*, Virago, London, 2006, first published in English 1954.
2. Noel Annan, *Changing Enemies: The Defeat and Regeneration of Germany*, Harper/Collins, London, 1995, p. 148. Grigor McClelland, *Embers of War: Letters from a Quaker relief Worker in War-Torn Germany*, Tauris, London, 1997; Sharif Gemie, Fiona Reid and Laure Humbert, *Outcast Europe: Relief and Relief Workers in an Era of Total War 1936–48*, Continuum, London, 2012.
3. Laura Blumenfeld, *Revenge: A Story of Hope*, Picador, London, 2002, p. 371.
4. Eamon Collins and Mick McGovern, *Killing Rage*, Granta, London, 1997, pp. 20–21.
5. Victor Nee and Don Layman, *The Cultural Revolution at Peking University*, Monthly Review, New York, 1969. Their book was dedicated to rebellious students everywhere.
6. Gordon A. Bennett and Ronald N. Montaperto, *Red Guard: The Political Biography of Dai Hsiao-ai*, George Allen and Unwin, London, 1971, p. 42.
7. Ken Ling, *Red Guard: Schoolboy to 'Little General' in Mao's China*, Macdonald, London, 1972, pp. 19–27.
8. 'Britain's forgotten allies who languish in refugee camps', *The Times*, 30 March 2013.
9. Lt-Colonel R. S. Stafford, *The Tragedy of the Assyrians*, George Allen and Unwin, London, 1935, p. 168.
10. Paul O. J. Hemphill, 'The formation of the Iraqi Army, 1921–33' in Abbas Kelidar, Editor, *The Integration of Modern Iraq*, Croom Helm, London, 1979, pp. 106–109.
11. 'Al-Qaeda pogrom may drive last Christians from the country', *The Times*, 11 November 2010; 'The faithful who must choose to walk in the shadow of death', *The Times*, 20 December 2010.
12. 'Most Christians flee after jihadist ultimatum', *The Hindu*, 20 July 2014.
13. For ingratitude in domestic politics see President Truman's comment that 'if you want a friend in Washington get a dog', quoted in Thomas C. Reed,

*At the Abyss: An Insider's History of the Cold War*, Random House, New York, 2004, p. 260.
14. William Shawcross, *The Shah's Last Ride: The Story of the Exile, Misadventures and Death of the Emperor*, Chatto and Windus, London, 1989.
15. John Hickman, *News from the End of the World*, Hurst, London, 1998, pp. 165–175. Andy Beckett, *Pinochet in Piccadilly: Britain and Chile's Secret History*, Faber and Faber, London, 2002.
16. John Major, *The Autobiography*, HarperCollins, London, 1999, p. 130.
17. Guy George Shane, 'The Establishment and Some Consequences of the Combined Threat Reduction Programme and Associated Programmes', unpublished PhD thesis, University of Cambridge, 2017.
18. 'Afghanistan's Hamid Karzai says NATO caused "great suffering"', BBC, 7 October 2013; 'Hamid Karzai's latest outburst at NATO is a sign of his deep frustration', *Guardian*, 8 October 2013. 'India helping in having our own army: Karzai', *The Hindu*, Madras, 15 December 2013.
19. See amongst his other writings, Nirad C. Chaudhuri, *Thy Hand Great Anarch! India 1921–1952*, Chatto and Windus, London, 1987 and Hogarth Press, London, 1990. But see the review in *The Times* by Karan Thapa, 'Myths of the Raj', 31 December 1987 and Chaudhuri's obituary, 2 August 1999. For another sympathetic Indian view of the Raj see also Kartar Lalvani, 'What did the British ever do for India? Almost everything', *Sunday Times*, 20 March 2013.
20. 'Taipei mayor's comments on benefits of colonisation draw rebukes', Focus on Taiwan, 25 January 2015.
21. Wei Wang, 'Chinese Policy Towards Protestantism since 1949: Historical, Ideological and Diplomatic Perspectives', PhD thesis, University of Cambridge, September 2012.

# PART II

# Responses

CHAPTER 5

# 'Memory Wars' and National Apologies

**Abstract** National apologies are one of the major diplomatic innovations of recent years and are meant to reduce feelings of victimisation and restore self-respect. They are not entirely rational and sometimes historically inaccurate but they can build confidence both between nations and between national governments and disadvantaged minorities. They have been made by the English-speaking countries to their indigenous minorities but repeated demands for apologies are also used as weapons between the East Asian nations exacerbating tensions between them. To be diplomatically effective apologies need to be undisputed otherwise they will do more harm than good.

**Keywords** Confidence • Minorities • Regret • Responsibility • Slavery

Diplomatic gambits have to be judged primarily by their benefits rather than their logic or historical sense. Faced with complaints of past suffering which their country has allegedly caused, democratic politicians have resorted increasingly to institutional apologies. They would have been less controversial if this form of words had not become the norm, if instead leaders had described certain past activities by their country as perhaps 'despicable' or 'lamentable'. Apology implies that individuals feel somehow responsible for historic events which have not been lodged in the

© The Author(s) 2018
P. Towle, *History, Empathy and Conflict*,
https://doi.org/10.1007/978-3-319-77959-1_5

national memory or for more recent actions by their government which they deeply opposed at the time. But an apology has become the norm and it would be hard if not impossible to change it now. In any case since the development of mass education, many people have identified with their nation and felt satisfaction at its achievements, technical, cultural, sporting, economic or indeed military. If Britons can identify themselves with Shakespeare's plays, Darwin's scientific breakthroughs or its sporting achievements, they need to be reminded of Britain's part in the slave trade, the repression of Ireland and the chaos left behind by their empire in Palestine and Kashmir. If they ignore their ancestors' failings they give the impression that they do not recognise the sufferings of other peoples and might indulge in the same behaviour again.

But the process is always something of an artificial political contrivance, a transaction between one people and another rather than individuals. The average Briton would regard the sender as unhinged if another Briton sent a message to him asking for an apology because the recipient's rich ancestor enclosed the common land in the eighteenth century which supported the senders' much poorer labourer forebears.[1] Yet enclosures must have caused misery and were bitterly opposed not only by the poor but by those writers most familiar with labourers' conditions. The dispossessed victims must have had to hitch rides on carts or trudge with their children and elderly parents many miles to one of the expanding industrial towns in the hope of finding work, lodging and food.

Demands by one state to another for apologies are akin to weapons.[2] They are meant to unite the demander's people, to denigrate the recipient's image and to make it less likely that it can find allies. Used by a weak minority within a state they are a defensive weapon intended to remind the government and the majority of the way in which the minority or its ancestors suffered in the past and to appeal for compensation or help to deal with current hardships. They are not intended to denigrate the country internationally, merely to 'put the record straight', enhance their often much diminished dignity and win justice as the minority sees it.

Chinese complaints about Japan's past behaviour illustrate the first or offensive policy. What shows their offensive nature is that they have intensified when many of those Chinese who suffered in the wartime years and those who inflicted such atrocities have already died. At the end of the Second World War hundreds of thousands of Japanese found themselves in China and entirely at the mercy of the Chinese people who they had so recently been repressing, killing or otherwise tormenting. Yet surprisingly, on orders from both the Nationalist and Communist leaders, despite these terrible memories the Chinese often treated their prisoners with restraint. In contrast, the Soviets, who had not suffered Japanese attacks, transported Japanese prisoners to Siberia where they forced them to labour in appalling conditions and where many of them died. According to Professor Hideo Kobayashi of Waseda University, 'men repatriated from China were sent home to establish a Sino-Japanese Friendship movement. It was for this purpose that the Chinese gave them such favourable treatment. As a result the Japanese prisoners were made to recognise their war crimes as well as forming groups to strengthen Chinese-Japanese friendship'.[3] The Chinese also needed technical help from Japanese engineers and continued to employ them in their mines and other industries.

By the early 1990s the position had completely changed. Japan had recovered from the Second World War and many economists mistakenly predicted that its GNP was likely to become larger than its US equivalent by the end of the century. Japan and India were candidates for permanent seats on the Security Council of the UN. But China wanted no such Asian rivals for status, it had only taken over a seat in the UN in October 1971 and it had no desire to diminish its own standing. While many Asian states, led by Japan, Taiwan and South Korea, had become success stories, the economic policy of the Chinese Communist party had failed and had cost the lives of countless millions of Chinese citizens. Under the leadership of Deng Xiaoping, the party turned in the 1980s to a much looser form of economic management which was to unleash the natural entrepreneurial instincts of the people. At the same time the communist party wished to maintain total political control, a determination strengthened in the 1990s when the Soviet Union fell apart after Mikhail Gorbachev's liberalising reforms. Thus, they used films, television and the schools to unite the nation by demonising the Japanese and creating a public demand for repeated apologies from the Japanese government. The consequences are clear in increased Sino–Japanese hostility. One poll published in August 2013 showed that just under half the Japanese people said that Chinese criticism of Japan over historical issues was a principal reason for their negative impression of China. Over 60 % of Chinese said that Japan's 'lack of a proper apology and remorse over the history of invasion of China' was the reason for their negative impressions of Japan. Of course, both publics mentioned the confrontation between the two states at that time over claims to ownership of the Senkaku or Diaoyu Islands but arguments over wartime history were almost equally important.[4]

Japanese governments have not helped the situation because they have often seemed half-hearted in their apologies for wartime events and government-mandated teaching in Japanese schools has appeared equally squeamish. But Chinese criticisms are in some ways exaggerated; Jane Yamazaki of Wayne University in the United States compared German and Japanese apologies for their country's policies in the Second World War and found them less of a contrast than many suppose. On the other hand, apologies have caused only muted controversy in Germany while in Japan they have been the source of continuous disputes and this has given the impression that many Japanese were either ignorant of the past or reluctant apologists.[5] On their side the Japanese feel persecuted today because it is not just the Chinese who demand apologies, South Koreans and others who suffered under Japanese rule in the twentieth century are also vociferous in their complaints. Unfortunately, repeated demands for apologies can excite resistance amongst the 'accused' group or nation and this has been particularly the case in East Asia. Japanese commentators protest that 'there is a behavioural pattern in South Korean politics that every time there is a change of government, a newly elected president, in order to seek public popularity, tries to make the Japanese Prime Minister of the time apologise'.[6] The result is that more Japanese have begun to dispute the historic accuracy of claims that their predecessors enslaved Korean and Chinese women, and committed countless other war crimes.[7]

As pointed out above, on their side the Japanese focus on the nuclear attacks on Hiroshima and Nagasaki. In recent years they have also found another cause of complaint, the kidnapping by North Korea of young Japanese from the beaches of Japan. There had long been rumours in Japan that such kidnaps had taken place but in September 2002, in an effort to put the past to rest, the North Korean leader Kim Jong-il not only admitted the kidnaps but declared 'the [North Korean] Special Forces were carried away by a reckless quest for glory. It was regretful and I want frankly to apologise. I have taken steps to ensure that it will never happen again.'[8] Although 'regretful' is a weak adjective to use in the circumstances, the apology was in other ways ideal; it expressed regret, admitted that the blame lay squarely on North Korean agents and promised that it would not be repeated. It must also have been a difficult apology for a North Korean dictator to make and especially to a country which most North Koreans disliked because of the four decades when it had ruled and repressed their country. But it had the reverse effect to that intended partly because it was a rare case where the apology confirmed what had earlier only been a rumour and because it included the admission that many of the young victims had died. Thus it exacerbated the sorrow of their relatives and showed that people could be seized from Japan and particularly from its coasts without the state being able to protect them. Relations between the two countries were deeply scarred although some commentators have seen the issue as a symbol of the poor relations rather than a cause.[9]

Apologies will never improve relations between nations unless the complainants want to be mollified but, if their motive is to denigrate the other state, then any number of admissions cannot be expected to do so. All the 'offending' government can do after it has apologised is to try to persuade its people to ignore the repeated complaints. The more their media respond to these, the more historians or commentators dispute the accuracy of the complaints, the worse the vicious cycle of accusations will become. In itself this may not cause outright violence between two states but it does prepare public opinion for such violence. Violence rarely occurs 'out of the blue', there is generally a period of rising tension and demonisation at least from one side beforehand.

In other circumstances a national apology or at least an acknowledgement of the suffering on the other side might well figure as a 'confidence building measure'. Soon after he became British Prime Minister Tony Blair offered an apology for the 'potato famine' in Ireland in the 1840s and it is widely held that this helped the talks which eventually led to the 'Good Friday Agreement' abating the violence in Northern Ireland between the Catholic and Protestant para-military organisations. Blair suggested that British governments had 'stood by' while people died during the potato famine. In fact, when the famine broke out Robert Peel's Conservative government authorised the expenditure of £600,000 on famine relief. By 1846 734,000 people were being employed on relief works and three million were being supported by public funds. £160,000 worth of maize was bought in the United States and sent to Ireland. In the end, relief measures cost over seven million pounds, though critics have pointed out that this was less than the compensation paid to slave owners in British colonies after emancipation in the 1830s or than the cost of the Crimean War which broke out a decade after the famine. However, the government was distracted in the 1840s because the famine coincided with, and played a major part in a convulsion in British politics which split Peel's party.[10] This, in turn, led to the establishment of a new Whig government which, wedded to laissez faire ideology did, indeed, 'stand by' to some extent while the famine proceeded. But dogma was not the only problem, the bureaucracy in Ireland was primitive and over-dependent on landlords, and policy was over-centralised in London.[11] Such historical detail is irrelevant to an apology of this sort which must appear unqualified if it is to be politically effective.

In March 1997 just before he became Prime Minister Tony Blair also condemned Britain's involvement in the slave trade.[12] At the time he was on a visit to Ghana and no doubt his comments pleased his hosts and would have been shared by all Western peoples. It would have undermined their diplomatic purpose to point out that slavery was endemic in Africa before the Atlantic slave trade began and that most of the slaves were sold to Europeans by African slave-dealers.[13] Africans rightly felt that their dignity had been undermined by the way in which their ancestors had been enslaved by Europeans. Nor would it have helped to remind his listeners that it was the British Quakers and Evangelicals who precipitated the ending first of the Atlantic slave trade and then of slavery in the British Empire. It is now accepted that all forms of slavery are wrong and that the Atlantic slave trade was abhorrent whatever the circumstances.[14] The point with these apologies is that they evoked relatively little controversy and that this is vital if they are to be effective diplomatically.

In fact there is always a good deal of quiet public scepticism about such apologies and it is important diplomatically that it remain quiet. This goes back to the actual terminology referred to at the beginning of this chapter. If the events complained about are distant the public generally think it is nonsensical to refer to them, if they are more recent people want to put the onus on the government in power at the time. An American who had been an opponent of the Vietnam War or a critic of the Anglo-American intervention in Iraq in 2003 would say that the leaders or the party in government were to blame. He or she might still well want those leaders to admit their mistakes but their apologies should be personal.

Unfortunately, leaders can rarely bring themselves to do so not least because the implications can be so horrifying. Selwyn Lloyd, who was Foreign Secretary when Britain tried to recover the Suez Canal from Egypt in 1956, claimed later that all the conservative leaders in Jordan, Iraq and the Gulf States would have been overthrown if the French, British and Israelis had not acted. It is very hard to see why this should have been the case, rather one could argue that, as friends of Britain or France, they became much more vulnerable because of the Anglo-French misjudgements and it was notable that King Faisal of Iraq was overthrown 2 years later.[15] Jack Straw, who was British Foreign Secretary in 2003, began the chapter in his memoirs about the Gulf War, 'I could have prevented the United Kingdom's involvement in the Iraq War. I did not do so. I chose to support the war. Here's why.'[16] There then follows a description of how he was sucked into playing a key role in the decisions which led to war by his loyalty to Prime Minister, Tony Blair, his belief that the containment of Iraq's ambitions was failing and by the government's hope of having some influence on the US administration. Mr. Straw's next chapter argues that the invasion of Iraq was a success and that it was the occupation (for which he says Britain was not responsible) that was a disaster. But there would have been no failed occupation if there had been no invasion and, as a consequence, thousands of Iraqis have died and in 2014 the country imploded in a genocidal civil war between Sunnis, Shiites, Kurds and the militants of the 'Islamic State'.

Major governmental policies almost invariably have unintended effects that they deplore. During the nationalist disturbances in parts of British India after the First World War, General Dyer, the British officer in charge of troops in Amritsar was not commanded to shoot demonstrators or rioters. Dyer was, however, responsible for keeping order in the town and, no doubt, he thought erroneously that this was the best means to do so in the turbulence facing him at the time. The result was the death of hundreds of the demonstrators and the growth of Indian hostility to British rule.[17] During the invasion of Iraq in 2003 British troops hooded and beat innocent civilians and killed the hotel receptionist, Baha Mousa.[18] On both these occasions many members of the government in London were, no doubt, appalled by what had happened and the wiser ones saw it as a public relations disaster equivalent to a military defeat. However, they had created the circumstances that made the disaster possible.

In other situations it was not the agents of the government who took the decisions that led directly to the mistreatment of other people. Many of the worst abuses in the slave trade and in the plantations employing slaves in the British Empire were carried out by private individuals though slavery as a whole was condoned by the British government until the end of the eighteenth century.[19] Do such gradations matter and how does one compare suffering caused by the agents of the government deliberately or by mistake with suffering inflicted by their allies or by fellow citizens? Similarly, one might ask whether a government should be more willing to apologise for an action which occurred 20 or 50 years ago than one which occurred 500 years ago?

Part of the problem with apologies lies in our confused attitude towards institutional responsibility. Banks are now frequently loaded with massive fines for the misbehaviour of some of their managers. But plainly a bank is made up of its customers, shareholders, counter clerks in the local branches, all of whom are made to pay for the misdemeanours of a few senior managers who often escape any sanctions. Similarly, the National Health Service in Britain is sued by patients who feel that they have been hurt by the service provided. Again, however, nurses, doctors and patients, and indeed eventually every tax payer, is being fined for the failings of the few. In criminal terms this is equivalent to fining or imposing a curfew on a particular town on the grounds that it has 'allowed' a murder or demonstration to take place there. Because it was so obviously unjust, collective punishment of such areas has long since ceased in democracies yet it has been increasingly employed against the institutions cited above.

Similarly, the idea of holding a whole nation responsible for the actions of its government has historically been rejected by those who believe in the notion of 'just war'. Jus in bello lays down that belligerent actions should, so far as possible, be directed against the enemy armed forces rather than against civilians. Such civilian casualties as may be caused unintentionally should be proportionate to the envisaged gains while prisoners of war and hostages should not be killed. Of course, one can argue that the concept is morally dubious because a German civilian in the 1930s might have been an ardent supporter of the aggressive and murderous Nazi regime whereas a conscripted soldier may have loathed the regime and been wholly opposed to its expansionism.[20] But, since it was impossible to make such distinctions in wartime, jus in bello laid down that war should be directed as far as possible against the armed forces and international law has followed its lead.

We know that demands for apologies and agreements by states to apologise are haphazard and distort memory. In other words, terrible suffering has been imposed on some peoples by others but the 'sufferers' have forgotten about it over the years or left it to historians to discuss; the French are not asked to apologise for the Napoleonic Wars which killed hundreds of thousands of people across Europe nor the British for the earlier Hundred Years War which devastated much of what is now part of France. Islamists complain about the Crusades but are less forthcoming about Ottoman repression of the Balkan peoples which lasted longer and only ended for the most part around the close of the nineteenth century. German leaders were very wise to show contrition for the cold-blooded murder of some six million Jews, gipsies and others in the Second World War but it is not clear that they have been equally apologetic about the millions of people the Nazis killed in the former Soviet Union, Yugoslavia and Poland. The communist parties in China and the Soviet Union have not apologised to their own peoples for the tens of millions murdered in their name. In itself this distorts history because many have come to believe that the Holocaust was the greatest mass murder in the twentieth century while, if the statistics in a recent history of Mao's rule in China are correct, only one of the man-made famines he caused there killed more than seven times as many.[21] What made the Holocaust particularly abhorrent was not just its size by twentieth-century standards but its cold-blooded, industrial methods carried out by one of the most advanced European nations, the fact that it was mainly directed against one people and that it was intended to obliterate them within Europe.

The peoples who suffered often have their travails much more firmly fixed in their memories than those who inflicted them. Much depends on education and the media. It is doubtful whether any but a tiny handful of Britons know about the Amritsar massacre or about the apologies made by their governments for other historic wrongs.[22] In contrast, memories of Amritsar are kept alive in India by media reports and by a film shown in 2000 of the life of the man who tried to avenge the massacre.[23] *The Guardian* reported in 1987 that a group of Indian lawyers, diplomats and politicians wanted an annual day of commemoration for those shot.[24] Because of their education most British people will know about their country's involvement in the slave trade and Germans will certainly be aware of the Holocaust. Similarly, Japanese will know about Chinese resentment against their country because of the Second World War but, because of their schooling, not of the details of the various massacres or the extent of the killing. The vast majority of Roman Catholics will not know that Pope John Paul 11 made over 90 apologies including ones for the involvement of Catholics in the African slave trade, the conquest of America and the religious wars following the Reformation.[25]

As pointed out earlier, pressure from disadvantaged minorities has to be distinguished from demands for national apologies which encourage international friction. The native peoples of Australia, the United States, New Zealand and Canada have begun to ask for legal, financial or territorial compensation for their wrongs and the recognition of historic facts. Their ancestors were traumatised by the tide of foreigners who overwhelmed them, they were infected by new illnesses, deprived of their livelihood, hunting grounds and land, and their culture was despised. It is hardly surprising that many sank into alcoholism and despair, and that to restore their dignity they now want recognition of their ancestors' sufferings by the dominant groups in their society. Recently there have also been warnings that some people might turn to violence and that this may have parlous economic effects. Douglas Bland, who was formerly an officer in the Canadian army, has pointed to the increasing radicalisation of some Native Canadians and the vulnerability of the mining industries on which the Canadian economy depends.[26]

In these cases, governments have begun over the last half century to respond appropriately. In New Zealand, Australia, Canada and the United States they have tried to reach land settlements with indigenous peoples to give them security and to compensate for past losses. They have also apologised for historic mistreatment. In New Zealand the Governor General normally signs legislation into law but, in 1995, the Head of State, Queen Elizabeth signed legislation acknowledging that the Maoris were mistreated after the Treaty of Waitangi in 1840. Their land rights were guaranteed in that Treaty in return for their abandonment of sovereignty but, subsequently, some three million acres were seized by the government and sold to settlers. In the 1990s the New Zealand government not only apologised but negotiated with Maori representatives on the terms of the compensation in land and reparations.[27]

In February 2008 Australian Prime Minister, Kevin Rudd apologised to the Aboriginal people 'for the laws and policies of successive parliaments and governments that have inflicted profound grief, suffering and loss on these our fellow Australians'. In particular he condemned the practice of taking Aboriginal children from their families to educate them in Western schools. Some 50,000 children had apparently been 'kidnapped' in this way between 1910 and 1970.[28] In June 2008 the Canadian Prime Minister, Stephen Harper followed suit apologising to indigenous people whose children had been seized to educate them in Western style schools where they were often mistreated.[29] Two years earlier the government had agreed to pay two billion Canadian dollars to those who had been seized. In 2010 Republican Senator, Sam Brownback read a US Congressional resolution to representatives of Native Americans which 'acknowledged years of official depredations, ill-conceived policies and the breaking of covenants' and apologised 'to all Native Peoples for many instances of violence, maltreatment and neglect' by the US government.[30] In each case there were those who opposed the land settlement or apology and felt that it was inappropriate or that it would encourage yet further demands. But fortunately there has not been a general backlash or pressure to revoke the deals made. Major controversies would have had the reverse effect to that intended by the governments and would have increased the anger of the native peoples.

Never before has there been anything like this spate of official apologies and demands for apologies.[31] Moreover it is unlikely that the number of demands will decline for years to come. The Iranians would, for example, like the British government to apologise for its interference in Iranian politics in the twentieth century.[32] It is not unusual for a relatively new or revived idea to become the fashion in the struggle to avoid conflict. After the traumas of the French Revolution and Napoleonic Wars, it was the idea of bringing leaders of the Great Powers together in a conference or concert to solve each international problem as it arose. At the end of the nineteenth century a number of treaties were signed between the major powers promising to submit their disputes to arbitration, and the Hague Peace Conferences of 1899 and 1907 spread the notion that disarmament was the way to end war or, at least, reduce its destructiveness. Such ideas remain important arrows in the statesman's quiver but they cease to arouse the same hopes as they did when fashionable.

National apologies for past events, sometimes centuries old, can easily be criticised for being illogical, ahistorical or even downright absurd. But so can confidence building measures of the type enshrined in the Final Act of the Conference on Security and Cooperation in Europe. Here were two groups of nations which had armed and fulminated against each other for almost three decades, yet it was hoped that visits by groups of officers or the presence of observers from the potential enemy at military manoeuvres together with other measures might change the prevailing atmosphere in however small a way.[33] Critics could have argued that close contact might even confirm the size of the threat and the malevolence of the enemies' armies. One could say the same of the law of armed conflict in general and restrictions on the use of individual weapons in particular. Soldiers do not invariably comply with laws against killing captured enemy soldiers and this may exacerbate hatreds. Similarly accusations that illegal weapons have been used increase the anger of the 'other side'.

When demands for apology are refused or offered half-heartedly then the complainant's demands may become more importunate. The Armenians have been complaining for decades about the alleged massacres of their ancestors by the Turks during the First World War. Ankara's refusal to offer an apology has simply kept the issue alive and possibly encouraged terrorist attacks on Turkish targets. The Turks say that the Armenian deaths were a result of their predecessors' attempts to repress an Armenian revolt when they were deeply embroiled in war against the Entente powers and that many Turks also died in the fight against the rebellion. But this is the sort of quibbling which exacerbates a historic controversy and is difficult to defend in the face of detailed descriptions of the massacre by the then US Ambassador to Turkey, Henry Morgenthau and others. Morgenthau was writing when emotions were still high but he quotes the then government of Turkey and its leaders to back his claims.[34] Either he and the consuls and others who wrote in the same vein were liars or the Turkish stance is akin to the Holocaust-deniers of recent times. If the Turks were more accommodating one cannot be sure whether the Armenians could be appeased but they have economic interests in improving their relations with Turkey.[35]

Politics and diplomacy are never entirely rational and rarely without difficulties or dangers. A summit conference between national leaders can build confidence between them but it can also worsen relations if it ends in confusion, disagreement and personal antagonism.[36] All these gambits act like flywheels accentuating convergence or divergence between states and peoples. As far as national apologies are concerned the most important argument one can use in their favour is that they sometimes act as confidence building measures between peoples. Equally, the worst one can maintain is that repeated demands for apologies exacerbate relations between states and indeed excite hatred between peoples. Unfortunately, some governments making such demands are only too well aware of this and are happy to unite their own people at the expense of international harmony.

## Notes

1. J. L. Hammond and Barbara Hammond, *The Village Labourer: 1760–1832*, Alan Sutton, Stroud, 1987, pp. 75–86.
2. According to one historian of propaganda, Philip Taylor of the University of Leeds, all propaganda is a 'munition of the mind'. See Philip M. Taylor, *Munitions of the Mind: A History of Propaganda from the Ancient World to the Present Day*, Manchester University Press, Manchester 2003.
3. Hideo Kobayashi, 'The post-war treatment of Japanese overseas nationals' in Philip Towle, Margaret Kosuge and Yoichi Kibata Editors, *Japanese Prisoners of War*, Hambledon and London, 2000, p. 172.

4. '9th Japan-China Public Opinion Poll', 13 August 2013, Genron NPO and China Daily.
5. Jane W. Yamazaki, *Japanese Apologies for World War 11: A Rhetorical Study*, Routledge, London, 2006.
6. Sugiura Masaaki, 'Revising the Kono statement carries Japan-South Korea relations into unknown water', Japan Forum on International Relations, E Letter 20 April 2014, Volume 7, number 2.
7. 'Teaching History: Chapter 10 in which democracies join in East Asia's history wars', *The Economist*, 5 July 2014, p. 52 'Japan retreats from sex slave apology', *The Times*, 17 October 2014; 'Japan and the War: Abe's demons', *The Economist*, 6 December 2014.
8. 'North Korea apologises to Japan for bizarre tale of kidnap and intrigue', *The Guardian*, 18 September 2002.
9. See Robert Carlin, 'Talk to me, later' in Philip W. Yun and Gi-Wook Shin Editors, *North Korea: 2005 and Beyond*, Asia-Pacific Research Centre, Stanford, 2006, p. 28.
10. T. A Jenkins, *Sir Robert Peel*, Macmillan, Basingstoke, 1999, pp. 123–136. Peter Gray, *The Irish Famine*, Thames and Hudson, London, 1995, p. 94.
11. David Thomson, *Woodbrook*, Penguin, Harmondsworth, 1976, pp. 156–170; Enda Delaney, *Curse of Reason: The Great Irish Famine 1845–52*, Gill and Macmillan, Dublin, 2012, pp. 109–116, 123–130.
12. 'Blair "sorry" for UK slavery role', BBC News Channel, 14 March 2007.
13. Herbert S. Klein, *The Atlantic Slave Trade*, Cambridge University Press, Cambridge, 2010, chaps 3 and 5.
14. See the first hand slave's account of the cruelties of the trade in *The Interesting Narrative of the Life of Olaudah Equiano written by Himself*, St Martin's Press, Boston, 1995. Stephen Farrell, Melanie Unwin and James Walvin, Editors, *The British Slave Trade: Abolition, Parliament and People*, Edinburgh University Press, Edinburgh, 2007.
15. Selwyn Lloyd, *Suez 1956: A Personal Account*, Coronet, Sevenoaks, 1980, p. 259.
16. Jack Straw, *Last Man Standing: Memoirs of a Political Survivor*, Macmillan, London, 2012, p. 361. See also Tony Blair, *A Journey*, Hutchinson, London, 1988.
17. Alfred Draper, *The Amritsar Massacre: Twilight of the Raj*, Buchan and Enright, London, 1985.
18. A. T. Williams, *A Very British Killing: The Death of Baha Mousa*, Jonathan Cape, London, 2012.
19. For a survey of the trade itself see David Eltis and David Richardson, Editors, *Routes to Slavery: Direction, Ethnicity and Mortality in the Atlantic Slave Trade*, Frank Cass, London, 1997. Slavery has taken many forms over the centuries and in some cases slaves had legal rights and were often

freed see Jerome Carcopino, *Daily Life in Ancient Rome*, Routledge, London, 1941, chap. 3 and Antony Andrewes, *Greek Society*, Penguin, Harmondsworth, 1971, pp. 151–153.
20. For the torments that the war imposed on anti-Nazis forced to serve in the German army see Ursula von Kardoff, *Diary of a Nightmare: Berlin 1942–1945*, Rupert Hart-Davis, London, 1965; Marie Vassiltchikov, *The Berlin Diaries 1940–1945*, Chatto and Windus, London, 1985.
21. Frank Dikotter, *Mao's Great Famine; The History of China's Most Devastating Catastrophe, 1958–1962*, Bloomsbury, London, 2011. For more favourable views of the subsequent Cultural Revolution see Guobin Yang, 'Alternative Genres; New Media and Counter memories of the Chinese Cultural Revolution' in Mikyoung Kim and Barry Schwartz Editors, *Northeast Asia's Difficult Past: Essays in Collective Memory*, Palgrave, Macmillan, 2010, pp. 101–128.
22. These included Mrs. Thatcher's 1990 apology for the Munich agreement which allowed Nazi Germany to take over the Sudetenland in 1938; David Cameron's 2010 apology for the killing of Irish demonstrators in Londonderry in 1972 and William Haig's 2013 apology for mistreatment of Mau Mau suspects in Kenya during the uprising in the 1950s.
23. Alfred Draper, *The Amritsar Massacre*; 'Resurrection of a patriot?' *The Hindu*, 23 January, 2000; 'How he lost it', *The Hindu*, 4 September 2005.
24. 'Massacre haunts modern India', *Guardian*, 13 April 1987.
25. Mark Gibney, Rhoda Howard-Hassmann et al. Editors, *The Age of Apology: Facing up to the Past*, University of Pennsylvania, Philadelphia, 2008, p. 259 passim.
26. Douglas L. Bland, *Time Bomb: Canada and the First Nations*, Dundurn, Toronto, 2014.
27. 'Queen to say sorry to Maori people', *The Independent*, 2 July 1995. Negotiations, nevertheless, continue on other issues such as ownership of rivers, see *The Economist*, 9–15 May 2015, p. 56.
28. 'Kevin Rudd's sorry speech', 13 February 2008 in http://www.smh.com.au/articles/2008/02/13 downloaded 2 January 2014.
29. 'Canadian Government apologizes for abuse of indigenous people', http://articles.washingtonpost.com/2008-06-12/world downloaded 8 December 2013.
30. http://www.nativetimes.com/index.php/index.php/news/tribal/3651 downloaded 8 December 2014. Kevin Gover, Assistant Secretary-Indian Affairs had made a particularly far-reaching speech in September 2000 on the occasion of the 175th anniversary of the founding of the Bureau of Indian Affairs condemning its mistreatment of Native Americans; see, http://www.tahtonka.com/apology.html. For a history of recent US policy towards Native Americans see George Pierre Castile, *Taking Charge:*

*North American Self-Determination and Federal Indian Policy, 1975–1993*, University of Arizona Press, Tucson, 2007.
31. English governments had periodically apologised to the people for overstepping their power; see Thomas Babington Macaulay, *The History of England from the Accession of James II*, Routledge, London, 1908, Volume 1, pp. 30 and 48.
32. Seyed Hossein Mousavian, 'EU-Iran relations after Brexit', *Survival*, October–November 2016, p. 86.
33. *Conference on Security and Co-operation in Europe: Final Act*, Cmnd 6198, pp. 10–11, HMSO, London, 1975. J. J. Maresca, *To Helsinki: The Conference on Security and Co-operation in Europe, 1973–1975*, Duke University Press, Durham, 1987.
34. Henry Morgenthau, *Secrets of the Bosphorus*, Hutchinson, London, 1919, chapter 24 'The murder of a nation' and Henry Morgenthau, *Ambassador Morgenthau's Story*, Gomidas Institute, Ann Arbor, 2000.
35. 'Armenian Terrorism; Revenge sought for Turkish "genocide"', *The Times*, 9 August 1981; 'Dido Sotiriou', obituary in *The Times*, 29 September 2004; 'Mothers threw their children in the lake rather than let the Turks have them', *The Times*, 22 April 2005; 'US genocide resolution threatens to wreck good relations with Turkey', *The Times*, 5 March 2010.
36. Gordon A. Craig and Alexander L. George, *Force and Statecraft: Diplomatic Problems of Our Time*, Oxford University Press, New York, 1995, p. 59. The authors describe such conferences as 'surely the most unfortunate invention of the new diplomacy'.

CHAPTER 6

# Historical Education

**Abstract** History teaching should incorporate disparate opinions and uncomfortable facts but the temptation with contemporary history is to do the opposite. Parents do not generally want their opinions to be challenged in the schools. The Vietnam War is, for example, still a profoundly upsetting and divisive subject in the United States which teachers have often tried to make anodyne. This makes the whole subject less interesting and less accurate. All the combatants in the Second World War have their own history of the period and these different versions need putting side by side to compare the various interpretations. They often disagree not so much on the facts but on the emphasis they place on the different features, the context and causes of this and other pivotal events. Taught sensitively but comprehensively history can be a confidence measure between previously hostile nations, taught one-sidedly or as propaganda it is a major irritant.

**Keywords** Controversy • Correctness • Israel • Japan • Vietnam

Teaching contemporary history is bound to be controversial when the children's own country is involved and suffering and its causes are their focus. Parents are not alone in worrying that the next generation is being 'brainwashed' into accepting opinions at odds with their own memories.

© The Author(s) 2018
P. Towle, *History, Empathy and Conflict,*
https://doi.org/10.1007/978-3-319-77959-1_6

Yet the aim should be not to instil pupils with a particular opinion about the past but to supply the skills to examine historic claims of victimisation and to assess opinion formers' contentions that 'history shows' one policy or another is the right one. In the past, teachers often avoided sensitive subjects altogether or gave a one-sided view but, if they do this, pupils will fail to see how easy it is to criticise with all the advantages of hindsight and how difficult it is to make political decisions. Thus, they will not understand why people acted as they did and leave unexamined their own ideas and prejudices. Finally, teachers who avoid controversy will not pass on the excitement of the subject and give students the critical skills they need in later life.

Children today imbibe political ideas when they are less than 10 years old from the media, their parents, contemporaries and schools.[1] They are easily excited by tales of the victimisation of their family or their group. Apologies and diplomatic compromises deal at the political and diplomatic level with the threat that historical memories can represent but the deeper problem is the way in which culture is formed and history is taught. New generations will shape the world by what they have learnt in childhood; what we teach them in schools and universities is of vital importance even if it will only form a part of their world view. History is so important and has the potential for having such an impact on children that no group can be trusted to control it, not historians, not history teachers, not the media, nor pressure groups and certainly not governments. It needs constant, widespread debate between them.[2]

One example of the political importance of the way in which history is taught today was given by Keith Barton of the University of Cincinnati in a study he published comparing the Northern Irish and the United States' systems in 2008. Barton reminded readers that the British system examined specific periods in greater detail and was more analytical than the chronological US system. The British put more emphasis on the sociological context of events and the US on individuals' contributions to US and foreign history. US school children explained change or 'progress' by inventions produced by particular people. Northern Irish children were less likely to see changes as progress and more likely to see them as due to social and economic circumstances rather than individuals. Barton admitted the influence of historical television programmes and films but felt that these reinforced the different educational approaches in the two countries. As he pointed out, the contrasting methods have political effects with Americans prone to explain poverty by personal inadequacy and the British by circumstances. Thus, the US system encourages the entrepreneurial spirit, the British is more sympathetic to the victims of the system but also less capable of encouraging national feeling and, he felt, more likely to leave a vacuum in which sectarianism could flourish in Northern Ireland.[3]

Some of this is surprising given that the British are more dependent on the state and thus, one would imagine, more likely to give it support. However, his conclusions were largely confirmed by a Pew poll released in November 2011. This showed that 58 % of Americans thought that freedom to pursue life's goals without state interference was more important than state guarantees that nobody was in need, while 35 % believed state interference was preferable. In Britain the figures were almost exactly reversed with 38 % preferring freedom and 55 % favouring state guarantees. Pew also found that 49 % of Americans believed their culture was superior to others while only 32 % of Britons thought of their culture in the same way.[4]

Given its importance it is not surprising that history has been fiercely contested territory ever since the First World War.[5] In the 1920s one major issue in Europe was how attitudes towards warfare and the new League of Nations should be shaped in the schools. Mona Siegel of Sacramento State University has argued that French teachers between 1918 and 1926 pictured Germans as inhuman aggressors and the French soldiers as courageous defenders of the homeland. After that date, under pressure from the teachers' union, the caricature of the Germans was dropped and French soldiers were represented as victims of 'war' not of the enemy. The détente between France and Germany was then at its height and the change in French curricula could be seen as a major confidence building measure. On the other hand conservatives argued that such 'propaganda' was disarming the nation despite warnings about German revisionism, cries that grew ever more strident in the 1930s.[6] Although this debate was more intense in France than Britain, a meeting of 600 representatives of British educational authorities agreed in 1927 that history was the 'key subject' and that children should be taught that the League of Nations 'was fruit long ripened on the tree of time'. Others, however, worried that teaching was being biased towards pacifism and that the League was a flimsy structure on which to build the nation's defences.[7] In retrospect, this was exactly the sort of subject that should have reflected both sides and forced pupils to engage with the problems of international trust and suspicion.

There is a low-key debate today about how far, if ever, teaching should be consciously biased to undo past victimisation. This is an issue in the United States over the treatment of Black people who, many argue, were underestimated in previous histories. But this could apply in many countries which have minorities who were discriminated against in the past. Indeed, it could be regarded as a confidence-building measure between the majority and minority. There are, however, obvious dangers. It is condescending as well as inaccurate and it can increase the resentment of the previously dominant group who feel that political correctness has too much influence. This was, no doubt, one of the reasons for the popularity of Donald Trump's electoral campaign in 2016.

If pressure groups dominate the debate on education they may push change so that the removal of previous bias and study of victimisation leads to distortions instead of giving contrasting views. In 1999 three academics from the Centre for the Study of Social and Political Change at Smith College tried to demonstrate statistically how US school textbooks had altered in the way they described Blacks, Native Americans and women over the previous decades. They pointed out that only one Black was given any coverage in the 1940s textbooks. He was picked out because his life illustrated the increasingly bitter debate over slavery which led to the civil war that devastated the United States in the 1860s. Dred Scott was a slave who lost his case before the US Supreme Court in 1858. He had argued that, although he was born a slave, because he had lived in a state where slavery did not exist, he had become a free man. By the 1950s the number of Blacks mentioned had increased to seven, to 20 in the 1960s and 93 in the 1980s. Not only that but, while the percentage of Whites mentioned in the textbooks declined and the texts about them were ever more critical, most Blacks were evaluated positively. In one text Olaudah Equiano, the Ibo whose horrifying autobiography of his life as a slave mainly in the West Indies and Britain had been widely published, received more space than Benjamin Franklin, James Monroe, Andrew and Lyndon Johnson and John Foster Dulles. Rosa Parks who achieved fame by one specific incident—refusing to give up her seat on a 'Whites only' bus, was given more space in one text than 75 % of the Presidents and other notables mentioned. It is possible that one person could have a major impact through a particular action but Lyndon Johnson plainly did more to strengthen US policy on civil rights than Rosa Parks, not to speak of his impact on other aspects of US life. The authors concluded that 'demographic proportional representation is not characteristic of the past; it is a contemporary view superimposed on the past and thus represents the essence of present mindedness.'[8] Again older children and students need to be confronted with the dilemma presented by the social benefits of offsetting deeply divisive historic prejudices set against the requirement to tell the truth about the past as historians understand it.

Ever since its birth the Israeli state has faced such fundamental dilemmas. In 2002 Elie Podeh of the Hebrew University of Jerusalem published a study of Israeli textbooks which argued that after the passing of the State Education Law in 1953 only 1.4 % of the time was allocated to Arab history and that the texts generally portrayed Arabs in negative terms.[9] He also referred to an international survey held in 1967 which showed that all ages of Israeli children, if they had to choose to become a foreigner, 'would least like to be an Arab.'[10] Podeh quoted one leading educator, Avraham Orinovsky as suggesting that the establishment of a Jewish homeland in Israel 'does not and will not undermine the local Arabs' economic or cultural development. This, despite the fact that Israel is neither the Arabs' national homeland nor [their] cultural centre'. As far as the teaching of the conflict between the Arabs and Israelis was concerned in the 1960s, Podeh argued 'there are indications that superintendents and teachers were familiar with a more complex reality of the conflict than the simplistic picture presented in the textbooks. The gap between what these educators knew and what they taught and wrote demonstrates that [they] felt an unspoken need to conform to the prevailing nationalistic atmosphere in Israeli society.'[11] The picture is further complicated by bitter disagreements amongst Israeli historians and between Israeli and Palestinian historians.[12] But this could be the basis of challenging history teaching if both Israelis and Palestinians were ever willing to try to break down their entrenched prejudices and to show how their conflict had emerged and how there were so many victims on both sides.

In 2000 Laura Hein of the University of Wisconsin and Mark Selden of Cornell argued that educators were increasingly coming under international scrutiny for the content of their history teaching. [13] As pointed out earlier, controversy has been most intense over Japanese textbooks on the history of the 1930s and early 1940s. Japan's neighbours watch any change in the treatment of this period to detect signs of reviving Japanese nationalism.[14] But in that case potentially constructive arguments about historical accuracy have long developed into polemics in which nationalistic feelings distort reality. When emotions are at their height and governments use history as an offensive weapon little progress can be made. But, if people on all sides were ever determined to reduce these feelings and build confidence between nations then they could try to change the attitudes of future generations. Conflicting historical interpretations need placing side by side. In the Sino–Japanese dispute one text could give the conventional Japanese line and the other the way Chinese and most foreign historians describe the impact of Japanese forces on China and the rest of Asia between 1931 and 1945. No other treatment can teach children how differently the past has influenced foreign nations and how variously history can be presented. Moreover, it would also show that conflicting views can be integrated because their differences are often due to selection not to fundamental disagreements about the facts.

Drawing parallels between different experiences will be misleading if pushed very far but can still provoke thought. Professors Fujitani, White and Yoneyama of Toronto University suggested in 2001 that the US bases in Okinawa established after the Second World War were not a defence of freedom against communism but a new form of colonial oppression. The bases' colonial status was, they argued, proven by the way in which they took over farmers' land and by the number of crimes committed by servicemen against local people.[15] On the other hand, such crimes would be seen in the conventional Western discourse as an unfortunate consequence of any military presence, foreign or domestic, whether in Germany, Britain or Japan.[16] The same authors argued that Korea was not 'liberated' in 1945 but fell, in the southern case, under US colonial control.[17] What is needed in these cases is definition of the meaning of 'colonialism' and an assessment of the influence the US has had over Japan and the Republic of Korea after 1945 as compared with the control the imperial powers had over their colonies in the nineteenth century. In that way children would have to think both about imperialism and about the policies the US has been pursuing since the Second World War.

It is not surprising that US teachers sometimes shy away from treating such controversial subjects and perhaps above all avoid focusing on the Vietnam War. Even when they do discuss controversial events they may try to avoid argument by making them anodyne. Thus, James Loewen of the Catholic University of America argued the textbooks in particular often minimised disputes. He compared textbooks that covered the Vietnam War by whether or not they printed famous photographs of the war—the little girl burnt in a US napalm attack, the Buddhist monk burning himself in protest against the South Vietnamese government, the national police chief shooting a Viet Cong suspect, the My Lai massacre by US troops and the escape by helicopter from the US Embassy in 1975. Only one of the 12 older textbooks he examined had even one such picture, that of the police chief shooting the prisoner, the rest avoided them all. Newer texts sometimes included one or two of the key photographs. Loewen also argued that the texts gave very inadequate coverage to the opposition to the war and its motives, and failed to assess the reasons why the US entered the war.[18] One could add that they needed to show the popularity of the war in the United States in the early stages particularly amongst the more idealistic parts of the population—the young and better educated—and the way attitudes changed as casualties and destruction increased.[19] It began as a classic example of vicarious victimhood and was regarded as a struggle against a rapacious ideology.[20] It was also seen in the light of the Anglo-French failure to protect Czechoslovakia in 1938, as well as the eventual victories against Nazism in the Second World War and afterwards against communism in Greece and Korea. Coverage of all sides of the argument might be disturbing for parents or grandparents of pupils who had lived through the war and had very fixed opinions about it but an approach that forced children to think about the issues and understand why people acted as they did would be by far the most beneficial.

Good history teaching gives children access to texts supporting opposing points of view and shows how variously events are perceived at the time. This is more challenging, more interesting and more accurate than simply presenting them with one viewpoint. Pupils see that historians disagree about the selection, interpretation and the emphasis placed on the facts. This is all the more important and difficult in areas riven by conflict such as Northern Ireland, Israel, East Asia and the Balkans. To the extent that teachers can equip children with such a sophisticated approach they reduce the simplistic, one-sided history often taught in the past. No doubt, this irritates governments, parents and other teachers. But it is the first stage to putting contemporary claims of past victimisation into perspective.

## Notes

1. Amiram Raviv, Louis Oppenheimer, and Daniel Bar-Tal, Editors, *How Children Understand War and Peace*, Jossey-Bass, Publishers, San Francisco, 1999; Defra Lemish and Maya Gotz, Editors, *Children and the Media in War and Conflict*, Hampton Press, Creskill, New Jersey, 2007; Helen Brocklehurst, *Who's Afraid of Children: Children, Conflict and International Relations*, Ashgate, Aldershot, 2006.

2. For past debates about education in general see Richard Hofstadter, *Anti-Intellectualism in American Life*, Vintage Books, New York, 1963, pp. 299–390.
3. Linda S. Levstik and Keith C. Barton, *Researching History Education: Theory, Method and Context*, Routledge, New York, 2008, pp. 300–331.
4. Pew Research Center, Global Attitudes Project, 'The American-Western European Values Gap', pp. 1, 5 and 6.
5. B. J. Elliott, 'The League of Nations Union and History Teaching in England: A Study in Benevolent Bias', *History of Education*, 1977, pp. 131–141; Peter C Gronn, 'An experiment in political education; "V.G.", "Slimy" and the Repton Sixth, 1916–1918', *History of Education*, 1990, pp. 1–21.
6. Mona L. Siegel, *The Moral Disarmament of France: Education, Pacifism, and Patriotism, 1914–1940*, Cambridge University Press, Cambridge, 2004, chapter four. For warnings in Britain about German revisionism see J. M. Spaight, *Pseudo-Security*, Longmans, Green, London, 1928; J. H. Morgan, *Assize of Arms: Being the Story of Germany and her Rearmament 1919–1939*, Methuen, London, 1945.
7. Elliott, *League of Nations*, p. 134. See also Alfred Zimmern, *Spiritual Values and World Affairs*, Oxford University Press, London, 1939.
8. Robert Lerner, Althea K. Nagai and Stanley Rothman, *Molding the Good Citizen: The Politics of High School History Texts*, Praeger, Westport, CT, 1999, pp. 70, 77 and 85.
9. Elie Podeh, *The Arab-Israeli Conflict in Israeli History textbooks: 1948–2000*, Bergin and Garvey, Westport, 2002, p. 33.
10. This was confirmed by later investigations which showed how early negative images of Arabs developed though in that case the researchers stressed the importance of television in shaping ideas. See 'Social judgements in Israeli and Arab children' in *Children and Media in War and Conflict*, pp. 287–291.
11. Podeh, *Arab-Israeli Conflict*, p. 34.
12. For a balanced review see Neil Caplan, *The Israeli-Palestine Conflict: Contested Histories*, Wiley-Blackwell, Chichester, 2010, pp. 221–244.
13. Laura Hein and Mark Selden, *Censoring History: Citizenship and Memory in Japan, Germany and the United States*, M. E. Sharpe, Armonk, New York, 2000, p. 10.
14. *The Economist*, 7 March 2015, p. 50; ibid., 28 March 2015, p. 60; ibid., 18 April 2015, p. 50.
15. Crimes were, not surprisingly, a continuing source of tension between the US and local people even though some pointed out that US servicemen committed fewer crimes than Japanese civilians. 'Rina's legacy', *The Economist*, 25 June 2016, p. 50.

16. T. Fujitani, Geoffrey White and Lisa Yoneyama, *Perilous Memories: The Asian Pacific War(s)*, Duke University Press, Duke, 2001, p. 13. For a different view see C. T. Sandars, *America's Overseas Garrisons: The Leasehold Empire*, Oxford University Press, 2000.
17. For a history of Korea see Ralph N. Clough, *Embattled Korea: The Rivalry for International Support*, Westview Press, Boulder, 1987.
18. James W. Loewen, 'The Vietnam War in High School American History', in Hein and Selden, *Censoring History*, pp. 150–171. See also Marilyn Young, 'Dangerous history and the "Good War"' in Edward Linenthal and Tom Engelhardt, *History Wars: The Enola Gay and Other Battles for the American Past*, Metropolitan Books/Henry Holt, New York, 1996, pp. 199–209.
19. Hazel Erskine, 'The polls: Is war a mistake?' *Public Opinion Quarterly*, 1970–71, pp. 134–149.
20. Robert Conquest, *The Great Terror: Stalin's Purge of the Thirties*, Pelican. Harmondsworth, 1971; Alexander Solzhenitsyn, *The Gulag Archipelago: 1918–1956*, Collins/Fontana. London, 1974; Frank Dikoter, *Mao's Great Famine: The History of China's Most Devastating Catastrophe 1958–1962*, Bloomsbury, New York, 2011.

CHAPTER 7

# Restitution

**Abstract** The existing geopolitical situation can rarely be changed to right historic wrongs and to do so would usually produce another group of aggrieved people. Massive change is thus rare but Norwegians and Swedes, Czechs and Slovaks divided peacefully and empires such as the Soviet Union have accepted their own demise. By contrast the Israelis and Palestinians dispute over the same territory and emphasise their historic suffering and humiliation. World leaders have devoted countless hours to finding some peaceful compromise but without success because of the nature of the dispute.

**Keywords** 1919 • Frontiers • Israel • Partition • Poland

If apologies fail to calm international resentments statesmen might turn to more radical solutions but these are naturally more difficult. Even when it is clear that a people's ancestors were infamously treated and that they are determined to overturn the status quo, one has to ask whether the current situation *could* be changed, what the costs of changing it would be, what the final consequences might be and whether the sum total of human happiness would be increased and misery reduced if the outcome of historical events were reversed.

© The Author(s) 2018
P. Towle, *History, Empathy and Conflict*,
https://doi.org/10.1007/978-3-319-77959-1_7

Of course there have been occasions when the status quo was changed relatively peacefully by mutual agreement; Belgium and the Netherlands were divided after Belgian rioting in 1830, Norway and Sweden became separate countries in 1905 and in 1993 the Czechs and Slovaks agreed on divorce. The English had learnt from their Irish experience in the 1920s and would not have thought of fighting for the continuation of Great Britain if the Scots had voted for independence in 2014. While many colonial powers including Britain tried initially to repress nationalists who disputed their rule, in the end they had to give way. 'Peace' was achieved in every case when the side which had been predominant recognised that it was no longer possible or too expensive to hold the political entity together.

It is not clear that these resolutions have generally left a legacy of bitterness on the side of the formerly dominant power except where minority 'settler' populations were victimised by the secessionist government, though Russia is one exception. Norwegians and Swedes do not glare across their mutual frontier, Czechs and Slovaks do not arm against each other. What distinguishes the feuds between Protestants and Catholics in Northern Ireland or Israelis and Palestinians is that any territorial repartition would leave anger on one side and possibly on both. In such cases violence may continue spasmodically for decades periodically taking the lives of innocent people. Other ways have to be sought in such cases to overcome the feelings of injustice.

Typically, major changes to state boundaries are made in war or in its immediate aftermath, but it is hard to introduce massive changes judiciously in such circumstances. The difficulties are exemplified by the efforts of the peacemakers at the Paris Peace Conference in 1919. The three dominant figures, Woodrow Wilson, Lloyd George and Georges Clemenceau were, despite all the criticisms which were made of them then and later, genuinely trying to sort out the problems created by the collapse of Russia, Austria-Hungary, Germany and the Ottoman Empire in ways that would improve the lives of the peoples living there. But they were under titanic pressure from the media and from clamorous peoples and interests to produce transformative peace treaties in a few short weeks.[1]

Historians and commentators have mocked many of their efforts; the Hungarians, Austrians, Italians, Japanese, Chinese and Germans all felt bitterly unsatisfied and unfairly treated. Even in Czechoslovakia, which was often held up in Britain as the most liberal of the new East European states, there were complaints from Hungarians, Slovaks and Germans that some within Czech borders were left stateless, that their language could not be taught in schools and that electoral districts were distorted to their disadvantage. New nations are often intolerant, particularly of formerly dominant groups.[2] Within months pogroms broke out in Poland and war between Poland and Russia; thousands of Greeks whose ancestors had lived for centuries in Turkey were expelled or killed.[3] Two of the new nations which were welded together, Yugoslavia and Iraq eventually collapsed and the Czechs and Slovaks agreed to divide their nations. Poland, which was re-established in 1919, was to be moved bodily westwards by Stalin at the end of the Second World War. It is impossible to change frontiers in ethnically mixed areas and, even more so, to 'move' large, settled populations without feelings of victimisation.

But this hardly discourages those determined to change the situation. The Argentines claim that the Falkland Islands belonged to them because they say they had owned them before 1833. But in 1833 much of North America and indeed Argentina was occupied by Native Americans; Poland, the Baltic Republics, the Ukraine, Italy and Germany were not sovereign states, the Habsburg Empire occupied a great swathe of Central Europe, while the Middle East and Balkans were largely part of the Ottoman Empire. Yet, as a result of the Argentine claim that the one event which took place in 1833 should be overturned, hundreds of young men died when their forces tried to seize the islands in 1982.

The difficulty of reducing historic anger and mutual feelings of victimisation is illustrated only too well by the attempts that have been made to overcome Arab–Israeli hostility. US Secretaries of State have been struggling, unavailingly, for decades to mediate between the Arabs and Israelis. After four wars and years of hostility President Sadat of Egypt surprised commentators in November 1977 by offering to go to Jerusalem to talk to the Israeli parliament about his ideas on peace between Israel and the Arab world. In the middle of the emotional speech that he made to the Israelis, which stressed the need to avoid sacrificing lives in yet another war, he argued, 'peace is not a mere endorsement of written lines. Rather it is a rewriting of history. Perhaps the example taken and experienced, taken from ancient and modern history, teaches that missiles, warships and nuclear weapons cannot establish security.'[4] Accordingly, peace could only be built on justice and that involved establishing a Palestinian state. However, the Israelis believed their history culminating in the Holocaust had taught them they *could* only protect themselves by guns and missiles. They also held that they were right to hold most of the lands they had conquered even if they were prepared to negotiate over some of the territories taken in the 1967 Arab-Israeli War. Implicit in their belief was that the majority of Palestinians could not share Israeli territories.

This was not the intention of the British when they promised the Jews a 'homeland' in Palestine in 1917 and as they reiterated in 1922, 'they have [not] at any time contemplated the disappearance or subordination of the Arab population, language or culture in Palestine'.[5] But the Palestinians objected to the Zionist project from the beginning and particularly when Jews flooded into the area after Hitler came to power in Germany. They saw that the local culture was being fundamentally altered with Jewish immigration, as indeed Zionists intended.[6] In 1936 the Arabs began a guerrilla campaign against the British authorities which forced the government to limit the number of Jewish settlers and to consider the possibility of separating Jews and Palestinians and partitioning the area. After the end of the Second World War and the horrors of the Holocaust the surviving European Jews tried to gain access to Israel. Even so, in the estimate of the existing population of the territory prepared by the UN in 1946, the only city with a Jewish majority in the whole area was Jaffa with 71 % of the population. The city with the next highest percentage of Jews was Haifa which had a majority or 53 % of Arabs. In the estimate of land ownership prepared by the UN the previous year no city was majority owned by Jews, Jaffa again being the highest with 39%.[7] Of course, it is unclear how long these ratios had existed and how many Arabs, as well as Israelis, had immigrated under the mandate. With relations between Jews and Palestinians deteriorating, with guerrilla attacks on the over-stretched British army and with their economy struggling to recover from the war, the Attlee government in London eventually 'handed the problem back to the UN' and left Arabs and Israelis to fight it out. Better organised, with more determination and more competence with modern weapons, the Israelis won the war and thousands of Palestinians fled. Israel was established on what had been Palestinian territory.

The results contrast with one of the other great expulsions that occurred around the same time, the expulsion of German speakers from Czechoslovakia, Poland and the former Eastern states of Germany. The sufferings of those expelled were horrific and many tens of thousands died but, except amongst those who witnessed them first hand, sympathy was muffled firstly because of the fresh memories of German aggression and revelations of the Nazis' victims. The novelist, Storm Jameson who did see those interned in Czechoslovakia was shocked to discover the slow starvation, the freezing temperatures, the filthy conditions and the diseases rife amongst them.[8] Hitler had used the German speakers in Czechoslovakia and Poland to destabilise those states in the years before the Second World War and the majority peoples would never again feel safe with extensive minorities acting as a 'fifth column'. Finally, as German and Austrian prosperity grew in the 1960s, those expelled were absorbed into the workforce. None of these considerations applied in Israel/Palestine.

The Palestinians were unwise to use violence against the Jewish immigrants and British soldiers in the 1920s and 1930s not least because then and later indiscriminate attacks alienated foreign opinion. They would have been better advised to follow the tactics being employed by Gandhi against the British in India. This is extremely difficult as Gandhi himself discovered because assembling large numbers of people together often results in violence. But with modern communications passive resistance is likely to be much more effective than it was in the 1930s because foreign opinion naturally favours the weak. Whatever their tactical errors, the Palestinians were not disgraced as the Germans were in 1945 and they were not absorbed into a prosperous community as the exiled Germans were to be. The international community would have been united against any signs of German revanchism, it was deeply and increasingly divided over Israel and Palestine with the United States strongly supporting Israel, with the Muslim world equally hostile and the Europeans torn between the two sides.

The inherent difficulties were well illustrated by the touching dialogue between the Egyptian writer Sana Hassan and the Israeli journalist and author Amos Elon, published as *Between Enemies* in 1974. Each set out to be moderate and to empathise with the other side. They agreed that each people were ignorant of the other and that they themselves had never spoken at any length to people on 'the other side'. Elon admitted that the idealism of some of the founders of his state had never been fulfilled, David Ben-Gurion, for example, had hoped for 'a model for the redemption of the whole human race'. However, as Elon saw it, such ambitions had been overshadowed by the Holocaust and then the unending struggle with their Arab neighbours. Hassan, in turn, argued that the Israelis should 'break free from their fixation with the past'; Elon replied that Arab textbooks were caricaturing the Jews and deliberately encouraging racial hatred. Over and again their disagreements about past and recent events became obvious.[9]

Some experts on negotiating techniques have argued that those involved should ignore apparent positions and concentrate on finding out what their interlocutors really want.[10] But precisely what the majority of Palestinians hope to achieve is unclear. While some Palestinians are willing to come to a compromise over territory, there are many who want to eradicate the state of Israel, hence the importance the Israelis have always attached to recognition of the current situation by the Palestinians and Arab states. In a 2007 Pew poll 45 % of Turks, 80 % of Egyptians, and over 70 % of Jordanians, Kuwaitis and Palestinians denied that it was possible to reconcile the existence of Israel with the rights and needs of the Palestinians.[11]

If one examines the more radical Palestinian position, under the criteria for reversal of historic events listed earlier, it is very unlikely that Israel could be overturned by force. The Israelis would never willingly give up their state and they have a powerful, albeit unadmitted nuclear force which they would be prepared to use to defend it. Israel also has strong diplomatic and military support from the US. It is not, therefore, surprising that in the 2007 Pew poll Americans and West Europeans said they hoped that it would be possible to reconcile justice to the Palestinians with the existence of Israel; 60 % or more of Americans and British and over 80 % of French and Germans held out hopes of this sort.[12]

But, if this proved wrong and Israel could be overrun, it is unclear that the outcome be any happier than the present one. It is very unlikely that, if hundreds of thousands of Palestinian exiles then took advantage of the situation to return to their historic homeland, the two communities would live in harmony together. They did not live in harmony in the 1920s and 1930s and there has subsequently been too much violence and bitterness between them. Alternatively, if the Jews were again sent into exile, the international community would simply have exchanged one group of exiles for another.

Imagine a house where rooms have mainly been rented by one family from a landlord. A family of refugees comes and rents a few rooms. Gradually it fills these rooms with its family members. Scuffles and then fights break out between the two families, the landlord tries to maintain order but eventually abandons the struggle and hands it over to the magistrates. The second family, which claims to have owned the house centuries ago, drives the first family out of the house itself and into the garden shed and garage. Children from the shed periodically throw rocks through the house windows and the second family respond by damaging the shed roof and putting more of their garden equipment in the garage. The magistrates who initially supported the refugees become increasingly divided. Ideally, they would find a house for the denizens of the shed but such houses are almost impossible to find and expensive, and it is not certain that people would want to move. And so the struggle continues ....

The feud between the Israelis and Palestinians is perhaps the saddest and best known of the historic quarrels over land ownership which trouble the world but Pakistanis share similar revisionist feelings over Kashmir and this has been one of the factors leading to Indo–Pakistan wars in 1947, 1965, 1971 and 1999; the Chinese government, with strong support from the Chinese people, has declared its determination to fight should Taiwan declare independence from the mainland. On the other hand, nearly a quarter of Taiwanese support independence and most identify themselves as Taiwanese rather than Chinese. In neither of these cases could the revisionist desires on one side be satisfied without increasing the bitterness of the other. Most past events cannot be undone and maps cannot be redrawn wholesale without creating further anger and often leading to war. Every country suffered periods of violence but with mass politicisation and historic memory this violence perpetuates itself. The sores of the past have to be healed by other means, even if these seem much more feeble, such as apologies, financial help and compensation, understanding and, in the end, forgiveness and forgetfulness.

In the Sino–Taiwanese case recent Kuomintang governments have worked hard to improve relations with the mainland by developing economic links and encouraging tourism but the majority of Taiwanese are very hesitant about such confidence building measures and voted against the KMT in 2015.[13] It would require very strong and able statesmanship on both the Palestinian and Israeli side to overcome the decades of bitter hostility between the two peoples. The Israelis might acknowledge that the Palestinians had suffered terribly and offer their sympathy for their plight. The Palestinians would have to accept that the past cannot be undone. The Israelis would need to agree that, however hard they tried, the Palestinian leaders could not eradicate the threat of terrorist attacks. Gradually the economy of the West Bank and Gaza might be opened to the world thereby building confidence and trust between the two nations. But such a revolution could only be produced by the sort of strong leadership which pushed the French and Germans towards reconciliation after the three wars between them that had brought such suffering and bitterness from 1870 to 1945.

## Notes

1. *Lord Riddell's Intimate Diary of the Peace Conference and After: 1918–1923*, Victor Gollancz, London, 1933; Harold Nicolson, *Peacemaking 1919*, Constable, London, 1933.
2. Sir Robert Donald, *The Tragedy of Trianon: Hungary's Appeal to Humanity*, Thornton Butterworth, London, 1928; Jorg Hoensch, *A History of Modern Hungary*, Longman, London, 1988, chap. 3. For a modern assessment of the peace treaties see M. F. Boemeke, G. D. Feldman and Elizabeth Glaser, *The Treaty of Versailles: A Reassessment after 75 Years*, German Historical Institute/Cambridge University Press, Cambridge, 1998.
3. Henry Morgenthau with French Strother, *I Was Sent to Athens*, Doubleday, Doran, New York, 1929.
4. Terry Golway, Editor, *Words that Ring through Time*, Overlook, New York, 2009, p. 374. Perhaps Sadat felt guilty about the Egyptian and Syrian lives he had sacrificed when he insisted on continuing the 1973 war after the initial Arab successes and despite pleas from Assad in Syria, the Soviets and the Americans. See Victor Israelyan, *Inside the Kremlin during the Yom Kippur War*, Pennsylvania University Press, Pennsylvania, 1995, chaps 2 and 3.
5. *Palestine: Statement by His Majesty's Government, Official Communique* No 2/39, p. 3, quoting the Command Paper of 1922, Cmd 1700.
6. Efraim Karsh, *Fabricating Israeli History: The 'New Historians'*, Frank Cass, London, 1997. p. 67.
7. Michael Adams, Editor, *The Middle East: A Handbook*, Anthony Blond, London, 1971, pp. 153 and 155.
8. Storm Jameson, *Journey from the North: The Autobiography of Storm Jameson*, Virago, London, 1984, pp. 187–194.
9. Sana Hassan and Amos Elon, *Between Enemies*, Deutsch, London, 1974.
10. Roger Fisher and William Ury, *Getting to Yes: Negotiating an Agreement without Giving In*, Business Books, London, 1991, chap. 1.
11. Pew Global Attitudes Project: Spring 2007 Survey, pp. 9, 118.
12. Ibid.
13. 'Poll find 52.7 % say Ma did not uphold dignity', *Taipei Times*, 13 November 2015; 'China and Taiwan in masterclass of face-saving at "treacherous summit"', *Sunday Times*, 8 November 2015.

## PART III

# Force and Memory

CHAPTER 8

# From Heroes to Victimisers

**Abstract** Governments that intervene to protect victims of conflict in the Third World often come to be seen as the victimisers themselves not least because they do not know enough about the culture and politics of the country where they intervene. This was as true of the United States' intervention in Vietnam as of later interventions in Afghanistan and Iraq. On the other hand, Western interventions in Sierra Leone, former Yugoslavia and Kuwait are often seen as beneficial. The question for outsiders is to see in advance when intervention might be welcomed and when resisted and possibly repelled.

**Keywords** Afghanistan • Iraq • Sierra Leone • Vietnam • Yugoslavia

Western governments are frequently encouraged by their media and impelled by their own historic memories, by their interests and culture to try to reduce victimisation in the Third World. They do not have to bow to media pressure but, consciously and unconsciously, it is no doubt another factor in their decision making.[1] Usually their urge to prevent changes in the status quo and their empathy for the victims of change exceed their expertise; they are ignorant of the culture behind such conflicts and what might be done to reduce them. They do not see themselves as colonial powers and victimisers yet that is all too easily what they come to seem. When they do so they retreat into isolation and thus their policy oscillates between the two poles of intervention and inactivity.

Dozens of new states were founded from the ruins of the colonial empires after 1945. However, it was more difficult for these states to establish stable constitutions than it had been for such countries as Britain and the United States which set up their legal and political systems over decades if not centuries and before much of the population had been educated and thus politicised. One reason for the new states' difficulties was that various groups within each told themselves competing narratives of victimisation. Thus, many of the post-colonial states were riven by instability and civil war. At the same time the suffering and destruction caused by these conflicts were broadcast across the world by the media. Television coverage greatly increased public demand for Western governments to become involved in such civil struggles.

The widespread anxieties culminated in the resolution of the UN's 2005 World Summit that governments were responsible for protecting their people against genocide, war crimes, ethnic cleansing and crimes against humanity. If they failed to do so the Security Council could decide to do whatever was necessary to bring the situation under control. Critics of this policy argued that it was a new form of colonialism, which appeared to justify intervention by the former colonial powers and failed to deal with the root causes of violence.[2] There was no certainty that military intervention by the greatest powers would be successful in imposing peace. In any civil war the side which was winning would resent outside interference and anti-colonial rebellions from Vietnam to Algeria showed that guerrillas could wear down foreign armies equipped with the finest weapons of their time.

When governments decide to intervene in foreign quarrels they often rely on just one or two recent events in their own country's history to show that their proposed action is both desirable in terms of their own national interest and morally acceptable. Few Western leaders or journalists know much about the historic culture of states embroiled in conflict. As Jeffrey Race, the author of one of the most insightful analyses of US involvement in Vietnam in the 1960s, commented 'widespread failure of understanding permitted a belief at higher levels of the [US] government in possibilities that did not actually exist, in turn leading to increased intervention. Such an insufficient understanding was just one consequence of the generally poor American preparation for dealing with Southeast Asia and the types of conflict likely to arise there. This poor preparation also revealed itself in both the contributions of the press and the academic profession in Vietnam ... not a single member of the foreign press spoke Vietnamese.'[3] All this meant that Intelligence about the enemy was inadequate and a conventional army with poor Intelligence is just a succulent target for committed guerrillas.

The problem is that Western governments and publics know a great deal about the overt consequences of foreign conflicts but little about their causes or about the extent to which their own intervention to separate the combatants might be opposed or welcomed by the population. This lesson was absorbed and the Americans who fought in the Vietnam War in the 1960s and early 1970s or watched it night after night on their television screens naturally feared their armed forces again becoming involved in conflicts in the Third World, criticised on every side for inadvertently killing women and children and unable to bring order even in a small and backward nation.[4] Those who set out to prevent victimisation themselves became seen as the victimisers. Four years after the unification of Vietnam under communist rule the Oxford military historian, Michael Howard suggested that the most important result was the 'virtually unanimous determination of the American people not to get committed to this kind of intervention again.'[5] Yet, so powerful were the cultural forces pushing for intervention that before the 1990s this unanimity was fracturing and there was open friction between Secretaries of State, who sometimes wanted US armed forces to be used more frequently and Secretaries of Defense who hoped to guard the military from obloquy. Such debates became public between President Reagan's Secretary of State, George Shultz and Caspar Weinberger, the Secretary of Defense. Weinberger suggested that forces should never be committed unless the US public was clearly behind the operation. Shultz argued that 'the lessons of Vietnam' should not be used to prevent the US retaliating or trying to deter such states as Libya and North Korea which backed violent attempts to overthrow the status quo.[6]

When Iraq seized Kuwait in 1990 President George Bush struggled to convince Congress and the American people that the US should use its forces to protect the Kuwaitis against Iraqi brutality by restoring their country's independence. While 78 % agreed with sending troops to discourage the Iraqis from spreading their empire into Saudi Arabia, the population was evenly divided about whether this force should drive Iraqi troops from Kuwait.[7] But, after US armed forces quickly scattered Iraq's armies and freed Kuwait without themselves suffering significant casualties, there were some who wanted to invade Iraq itself and unseat its ruler, Saddam Hussein.

Bush and British Prime Minister, John Major opposed continuing the war into Iraq not least because they would then be left with responsibility for maintaining order there. For them the memories of Vietnam still loomed large because they had learned the lesson from history that foreign troops are rarely welcomed in a country and that, if widespread guerrilla resistance occurs, it will be hard, if not impossible, for the interveners to succeed.[8] In fact this was a lesson that has to be periodically recalled in the modern world; after the Spanish guerrilla uprising against Napoleon's forces at the beginning of the nineteenth century statesmen could already see the dangers of trying to occupy another country. When Napoleon's forces were defeated in 1813 allied leaders hesitated to invade France in case the French nation rose against them.[9] When they finally destroyed the Napoleonic regime in 1815 the Duke of Wellington, who was in command of their occupying forces in France, tried to make the burden as light as possible and shuffled the occupiers out of the country as soon as he could.[10]

Under Bush's successor, Bill Clinton the struggle between the interventionists and the Pentagon was symbolised by the arguments between the Secretary of State, Madeleine Albright and Colin Powell the Chairman of the Joint Chiefs of Staff over involvement in the civil wars which raged as Yugoslavia began to collapse in the early 1990s. This time there was the added twist that Albright was born in Czechoslovakia and thus had a very clear idea of the vulnerability of small states lacking outside help while Powell had experienced the Vietnam War and its devastating effect on military, and indeed national, morale.[11] Famously, when Powell warned against the possible dangers of becoming bogged down in the war raging in Bosnia between Serbs, Croats and Bosniaks, Albright asked him what 'this superb military' was being saved for if it was not to be used and argued that 'the lessons of Vietnam could be learned too well'.[12] Albright harked back to the failed appeasement policies of the 1930s to justify US involvement. She claimed that a failure to intervene on behalf of the Bosniaks would have similar results to Neville Chamberlain's abandonment of Czechoslovakia to the Nazis in 1938.[13] However Bosnia was not threatened by a great power, such as Nazi Germany, but by other parts of the former Yugoslav nation. Moreover, those who urged caution were not afraid that their forces would be attacked by the Serb army but of being sucked into internecine quarrels and guerrilla warfare.

Given their long and often unsuccessful experience of fighting insurgents, the British and French governments were also concerned about becoming involved in a guerrilla war when they committed their forces to peacekeeping operations in Bosnia. They, in turn, were lambasted by interventionists for using insufficient force and misunderstanding the lessons of history. The British government came under great media and public pressure to use their troops against the Bosnian Serbs who were generally seen as the victimisers of the Muslims in the Bosnian conflict. Leading articles in *The Times*, *Guardian* and *Independent* attacked the government for confining troops to peacekeeping. *The Independent* devoted its whole front page on two occasions to the names of prominent individuals in favour of enforcing peace on the combatants.[14]

Despite the reservations expressed by Powell and other Americans, the administration pressed for air attacks on the Serbians who they saw as the aggressors. The military advice given to the British government was that these would be unlikely to be effective because of the terrain and would end peacekeeping and humanitarian help to the civilian population. Intervention might also plunge their peacekeeping forces into a general war.[15] However, when the administration finally had its way and launched air attacks against the Serbs, this was the main factor which compelled them to negotiate a compromise peace at Dayton in October 1995. Some commentators pointed out that the growing effectiveness of Bosnian and Croat ground forces also played a role but US confidence undoubtedly increased, particularly in the efficacy of airpower. This tendency was further enhanced between March and June 1999 when another NATO air campaign against Serbia effectively forced it to abandon its hold on Kosovo without losses to allied forces.[16]

Thus, by the time al Qaeda terrorists attacked the Twin Towers in New York and the Pentagon in Washington in September 2001, the fear of becoming embroiled in an insurgency equivalent to the Vietnam War had become still further attenuated. The attacks also infuriated the US public as innocent Americans were now the victims. Thus George W. Bush's administration decided to intervene in Afghanistan to overthrow the Taliban government there which had provided sanctuary to al Qaeda's leader Osama bin Laden. In conjunction with the anti-Taliban forces of the Northern Alliance US air power and Special Forces initially proved decisive, the Taliban were driven from Kabul and a more amenable government installed under President Karzai. But, just as John Major and George Bush had feared would happen if they invaded Iraq in 1991,

US-led NATO forces became ever more deeply involved in Afghan affairs and the problems were compounded when the US and Britain invaded Iraq in 2003. Everything that had been learnt about the dangers of misunderstanding foreign cultures and becoming embroiled in guerrilla warfare had been ignored or forgotten.[17] Years of indecisive conflict, huge expenditure, extensive casualties and reports of soldiers torturing or killing civilians followed.[18] The Western nations had again become seen as victimisers not victims. The trauma was not perhaps as great as that left by the Vietnam War but the pendulum swung towards isolation, both the British and American governments drew back from intervening in the Syrian civil war in 2013 in the face of public and Parliamentary or Congressional opposition.[19]

A summary of their research published by the American Pew organisation in March 2011 showed how the US public had reacted to foreign victimisation over the previous 16 years. In June 1995 64 % of Americans denied that their country had a responsibility to stop the fighting between Serbs and Bosniaks. However, building on the success of the air campaign there and, no doubt, the previous war against Iraq, 47 % told Pew in March 1999 that they felt the US had responsibility to prevent ethnic fighting in Kosovo against 46 % who were still sceptical. By December 2006 51 % said their country had responsibility to stop the 'ethnic genocide' in Darfur against only 36 % of sceptics. However, in March 2011 after years of frustration in Afghanistan and Iraq, the balance had swung back to what it had been in June 1995 with 27 % accepting responsibility for stopping the civil war then raging in Libya against 63 % who were sceptical.[20]

Intervention in Afghanistan was, of course, unusual because it was a response to the attacks by al Qaeda on 9/11 and the US itself was the victim not a foreign nation. How difficult it would have been for the administration to make a limited response was shown by the criticisms of Barak Obama's subsequent administration. Obama used military power as a scalpel rather than a bludgeon, sending Special Forces to kill Osama bin Laden, the author of 9/11 in May 2011. He also ordered attacks on terrorists with drones in Pakistan and Yemen and deployed aircraft, Special Forces and advisors to Syria and Iraq to help in the fight against the Islamist organisation, ISIS. Yet widespread popular support for Donald Trump, the Republican candidate for the 2016 presidential election, when he promised to obliterate ISIS and 'make the US great again', reflected the demand, particularly amongst poorer, white Americans for a much more unilateralist and forceful response to world affairs. Obama was also blamed by commentators elsewhere including Britain for the chaos in Syria and Libya.[21]

The initial British reaction to these events largely paralleled American. Support for the US interventions increased during the 1990s with US successes in Iraq and former Yugoslavia but also, in the British case, because of events in Sierra Leone. In the 1990s that former British colony collapsed into chaos with torture, rape, mutilation and murder by various factions. Interventions to stop the fighting by African troops, by the United Nations and by a private military company all ran into difficulties. The general British opinion was that the introduction of substantial British forces in May 2000 proved more effective. Such forces helped UN troops stabilise the situation by defeating the various violent factions and cutting off the trade in diamonds which had funded their operations.[22]

In 2009 Andrew Dorman of King's College, London wrote a generally complimentary history of the operation which he called *Blair's Successful War* although he warned that it was deceptively easy because the opposition was much weaker than it became in Afghanistan and the Middle East. Moreover, it was fortunate that the British officer in command happened to be 'familiar with region, its politics and the relevant individuals'.[23] However the British government came to see Sierra Leone as too much of a pattern when considering intervention in Afghanistan and Iraq. In these cases, national hostility to outside intervention was much greater and nationalism was strengthened by religious animosity towards the invaders. Thus, like their US equivalents, the British public turned against interventionism as a whole and such feelings were increased by the 2008 financial crisis which left the government struggling with a budget deficit exacerbated by the wars in Afghanistan and Iraq. One author claimed that the Afghan War alone cost the British taxpayer £40 billion though Mike Clarke, Director of the Royal United Services Institution in London suggested that Iraq and Afghanistan together cost £29 billion.[24]

The truth is that there were good historical reasons for not intervening in *any* of these conflicts in Sierra Leone, Afghanistan, Iraq or former Yugoslavia despite the sufferings of the people of these countries. Most importantly, the Western nations had abandoned their empires after the Second World War because, as pointed out earlier, with world-wide politicisation they proved far too difficult and expensive to hold against local opposition. Both France and Portugal which tried for years to hold their

African territories found their demoralised armed forces bitterly divided and involved in attempts to overthrow their own governments.[25]

Yugoslavia, Afghanistan and Iraq had a history of resistance to outsiders and of great brutality. Contrary to some commentaries, the British usually had little difficulty invading Afghanistan in the nineteenth century and scattering its armies. What they found impossible was occupying the country for any length of time. The best they could do from their point of view was to support an Afghan ruler who was even more determined than they were to maintain Afghanistan as a buffer state between British India and Russia, and to sustain order in the country. Thus, they tolerated the ferocious Abdur Rahman who was Emir from 1880 to 1901. Rahman boasted to the rare English visitors that he had killed 120,000 of his own citizens to 'maintain order' and that he kept the mullahs under tight control. When Lord Curzon visited him the Emir told his British visitor that 'after one unsuccessful rebellion [against him] he had many thousands of the guilty tribesmen blinded with quicklime, and spoke to me of the punishment without a trace of compunction. Crimes such as robbery or rape were punished with fiendish severity. Men were blown from guns, or thrown down a dark well, or beaten to death, or flayed alive.'[26] Victims there were in plenty but the British public knew little about them and had had enough of interventions in Afghanistan. Rahman's successors were less ferocious but, perhaps as a consequence, none of them died peacefully inside the country before the US invasion in 2001, the others were murdered or driven into exile.

Iraqis resisted violently when the British were given the League mandate for their country after the First World War. It was only with difficulty that General Haldane restored order and the Kurds, in particular, continued to oppose British rule.[27] Iraqi resistance was so tough that it changed British strategy in the 1920s and 1930s. Subsequently London relied on the Royal Air Force rather than the army to maintain order in Iraq and in some other predominantly rural areas principally because it was cheaper.[28] Even then London found it wise to grant independence to the country under King Faisal only a decade later. Faisal's pro-British successor and his advisors were torn to pieces by the Baghdad mob in 1958 and the dismembered body of Faisal's influential uncle was paraded round the streets.[29] There was every reason to think in 2003 that, with the politicisation of populations and the growth of nationalism outside Europe and the Americas, violent opposition to foreign intervention would have increased over the following years.[30]

After the failure of the Serbs to resist NATO intervention in 1994 and 1997, writers sometimes belittled the struggles waged by the Yugoslav partisans during the Second World War. The journalist and historian, Max Hastings commented, 'Yugoslav partisans were the most numerous and pestilent of the insects buzzing about the open wounds of the Axis in decay, but their role was slight alongside of the Allied armies.'[31] Slight in comparison with the contribution made by the Great Powers it may have been but the partisans were not dismissed when Yugoslavia began to fall apart in the 1990s. The standard histories of guerrilla warfare at the time had been published by the former US Marine, Robert Asprey in 1975 and the Director of the Institute of Contemporary History in London, Walter Laqueur in 1977, both no doubt inspired by US experience in Vietnam. Their chapters on the communist partisans in Yugoslavia were based on accounts by German military, by allied officers parachuted into the Balkans to assist the partisans and by the guerrillas themselves. Asprey concluded from these that, 'without Tito's partisans, the Germans could have enjoyed an easy occupation. As it was, until the autumn of 1943, the guerrilla threat forced Germany to keep nine Wehrmacht divisions in Yugoslavia, a hefty force buttressed by ten Italian divisions and numerous Bulgarian and local quisling units'.[32] These, in turn, had to be strengthened as allied supplies to the partisans increased. According to Laqueur, 'Yugoslavia is one of the few cases in history in which a partisan movement liberated a country, and seized power largely without outside help'.[33] The partisans had sacrificed thousands of their fellow citizens in the struggle making up some 10 % of the total Yugoslav population.[34] Nor was there any reason to believe that airpower offered a quick and easy way to defeat guerrillas given the abject failure of US airpower in the Vietnam War in the 1960s and 1970s. By the time they withdrew from Vietnam in 1973 the Americans had lost 3221 fixed wing aircraft and 4587 helicopters.[35] To give some idea of the magnitude of these figures, at that time the British, French and German air forces had less than 1500 front-line aircraft between them.[36]

There was every reason to avoid involvement in such a maelstrom in 1992 yet the US bombing campaigns in Bosnia and Serbia proved successful while intervention in Afghanistan was to be costly and apparently futile and the 2003 intervention in Iraq was nothing short of catastrophic for the people there. The problem is to decide, in retrospect, why airpower was successful against Serbian forces in Bosnia and in Kosovo and why air and ground forces were ultimately ineffective in Afghanistan and Iraq, and whether Western governments should have known this would be the case beforehand?

The various national leaders in the resisting countries naturally played important roles but, in Iraq and Afghanistan, they were transient. In contrast, Radovan Karadzic, the leader of the Bosnian Serbs and Slobodan Milosevic, the Serb leader gave way in the face of Western airpower so that neither in Bosnia nor in Kosovo were NATO forces faced with a major ground war to supplement their air campaign. On the other hand, when the Taliban had been defeated in 2002 and when Western ground and air forces remained in Afghanistan, guerrilla resistance gradually increased. Similarly, in Iraq, long after the country's conventional forces had been dispersed and their leader Saddam Hussein had been captured, guerrilla resistance against the US forces and the incipient Western-backed government in Baghdad expanded and the fragmentation of the country grew apace.

The question then is why the Serb people did not continue their wars in Bosnia and Kosovo after their leaders gave up the struggle, while the Afghans and Iraqis persisted? The crux was that the Serbs felt they belonged to European culture and religion, wanted to be on good terms with the West and to join NATO and the European Union. They knew that they would not be mistreated if they abandoned the struggle; indeed with Western financial help, Serb cities were rebuilt after the Kosovo conflict. The ones who continued to suffer were those leaders who could be arraigned for war crimes before the Hague court and those ordinary civilians who had fled their homes and still felt it was unsafe to return. If the Serb confrontation with NATO had been prolonged Belgrade would have had nowhere to turn to except Moscow and for all their historic links with Russia, the experience of the Cold War had given the Serbs good reason not to want to be isolated or dependent on Moscow's goodwill. But Afghans and Iraqis had no such feelings; their culture and religion were wholly different from the Western invaders and their history was of resistance to outside intervention. Nationalism was discredited in Europe because of the two World Wars while it was growing in the Third World.[37]

Not only are there significant differences between nations but in some cases the differences are becoming greater. Because of the constant instability it is hard to assess Afghan opinion but Pakistan, Afghanistan's neighbour, has some cultural similarities and is accessible to constant polling. Yet there are still difficulties, the polls show that even when Pakistanis and Western publics appear to agree on the advantages of something like democracy they may mean very different things or rate them with varying degrees of importance. In October 2014 70 % of Pakistanis had positive feelings about Saudi Arabia, hardly a bastion of democracy, against 10 % who had positive feelings about India and 6 % about the United States, the two largest states which would be regarded in the West as democracies[38]; over 50 % of Pakistanis were saddened by the killing of Osama bin Laden by US special forces and 44 % believed he was a martyr. Forty-nine percent said bin Laden was not killed in Abbottabad where he was alleged to have been assassinated although 68 % felt the US infringed Pakistani sovereignty by carrying out the operation.[39] When asked what was their country's most important achievement since independence the largest proportion or over a quarter of Pakistanis said the development of nuclear weapons, it would be doubtful whether people living in any of the three Western nuclear powers would say the same or indeed even remember it as amongst their country's achievements.[40]

According to US President George W. Bush, the 20th century ended with a 'single surviving model of human progress, based on non-negotiable demands of human dignity, the rule of law, limits on the power of the state, respect for women and private property and free speech and equal justice and religious tolerance'.[41] Thus the US has tried to spread these values when its forces have intervened abroad in Afghanistan and Iraq. However, many Afghans and Iraqis might not want legal restraints on their ability to 'discipline' their wives and children or stop people criticising their religion and Prophet. Certainly, the proportion of Pakistanis who believe that parents should choose their children's careers and their daughter's husband has been increasing.[42] Over half believe that women are treated better in Eastern than Western society and over 60 % believe that Sharia should be the only law of the land.[43] Plainly they disagree with Western ideas of human dignity, the meaning of equality for women and justice.

Serbia in the 1990s did not, therefore, prove analogous to the case of Sierra Leone, or the examples of Afghanistan and Iraq, and indeed subsequently of Libya and Syria. Western forces could easily defeat the conventional armies fielded by such countries and expel or destroy their governments. But that compounded their problems; whether their armies stayed in the country for several years as they did in Afghanistan and Iraq or took little further part in the situation as they did after their aircraft helped rebels defeat Colonel Gaddafi's forces in Libya in 2011, the outcome was the same. They could only create chaos and leave anarchy behind. Far from reducing victimisation they compounded the suffering.[44] Western critics of their government's inaction when massacres took place in the Third World have often claimed that their reluctance to become involved in such cases was due to racism and to prioritising Western over other lives. However, the Serbian example would suggest that there were good cultural reasons why they should make a distinction between intervention to stop victimisation in Europe and intervention in the Islamic world and elsewhere.

Each event is indeed unique but, when considering intervention to prevent victimisation and overthrow repressive regimes US and British leaders allowed more recent experience in Sierra Leone, Bosnia and Kosovo to obscure the implications of the Vietnam War propounded by Jeffrey Race and by Michael Howard. Above all they forgot the need to study 'the culture and problems of the society with which they were dealing'.[45] In the conclusion to his history of Western interventions Gary Bass stressed the enormity of the suffering in a country rather than the practicality of intervention when a decision is taken to interfere. But intervention that fails, however good the intention, can only compound the problems and the feelings of victimisation.[46] While practicality is essential only very insightful experts on Serbia, Sierra Leone, Afghanistan, Libya and Iraq would have known that their peoples would take differing courses when their armies were defeated by the US and its allies. Only the shrewdest of statesmen would pick advisers who had such abilities and wide knowledge of past experience. They would also need to be willing to ignore their own intuitions and experience. In Britain's case the depreciation of Foreign Office influence and its replacement by advice given by journalists and political advisors chosen by Downing Street has considerably reduced the expertise brought to bear on such decisions.[47] Yet in the cases analysed above, and in many others, governments have been faced with choices that could mean life or death for hundreds of thousands, traumas which may trap peoples in memories of historic victimisation and so be influencing events long after all involved in these recent wars have died.

## Notes

1. Nick Gowing, 'Media coverage: Help or hindrance in conflict prevention?' in Stephen Badsey, Editor, *The Media and International Security*, Frank Cass, London, 2000, p. 204.

2. Mojtaba Mahdavi, 'A post-colonial critique of responsibility to protect in the Middle East', *Perceptions: Journal of International Affairs*, Spring 2015, pp. 7–28. Mahdavi is Professor of Islamic Studies at the University of Alberta.
3. Jeffrey Race, *War Comes to Long An: Revolutionary Conflict in a Vietnamese Province*, University of California Press, Berkeley, 1972, pp. ix–x. See also the essays by Hans Morgenthau reproduced in *Essays of a Decade: 1960–1970*, Pall Mall Press, 1970, pp. 398–425 and the excellent study of the problem by Ken Booth, *Strategy and Ethnocentrism*, Croom Helm, London, 1979.
4. See, for example, Colin Powell with Joseph Persico, *My American Journey*, Ballantine, New York, 1996, pp. 120, 143, 248.
5. Michael Howard, '"Many reasons" for Vietnam', *Encounter*, May 1979, p. 24.
6. George P. Shultz, *Turmoil and Triumph: Diplomacy, Power and the Victory of the American Ideal*, Scribner, New York, 1993, pp. 646, 650, 286 and 106.
7. 'Americans believe US participation in Gulf War a Decade Ago Worthwhile', Gallup News Service, 26 February 2001.
8. John Major, *The Autobiography*, Harper/Collins, London, 1999, p. 240. Douglas Hurd, *Memoirs*, Little Brown, London, 2003, pp. 453–454.
9. Adam Zamoyski, *Rites of Peace: The Fall of Napoleon and the Congress of Vienna*, Harper/Collins, London, 2007, p. 148.
10. T. D. Veve, *The Duke of Wellington and the British Army of Occupation in France, 1815–1818*, Greenwood Press, Westport, 1992.
11. Powell, *American Journey*, loc cit; David Halberstam, *War in a Time of Peace: Bush, Clinton and the Generals*, Bloomsbury, London, 2002.
12. Madeleine Albright, *Madam Secretary: A Memoir*, Macmillan, London, 2003, pp. 182, 184, 405–407.
13. Albright, *Madam Secretary*, p. 192.
14. 'The British debate about intervention in European conflicts' in Lawrence Freedman, Editor, *Military Intervention in European Conflicts*, Blackwell Publishers, Oxford, 1994, p. 100. See also, Brendan Simms, *Unfinest Hour: Britain and the Destruction of Bosnia*, Allen Lane, The Penguin Press, London, 2001, pp. 342–345 and especially 349.
15. Hurd, *Memoirs*, pp. 499, 502 and 504.
16. International Institute for Strategic Studies (hereafter IISS), *Strategic Survey 1994/5*, London, May 1995, pp. 93–105; IISS, *Strategic Survey 1995/6*, London April 1996, pp. 126–138. See also Major, *Autobiography*, pp. 532–549; Hurd, *Memoirs*, p. 526.
17. David Kilcullen, *The Accidental Guerrilla: Fighting Small Wars in the Midst of a Big One*, Hurst, London, 2009; Emile Simpson, *War from the*

*Ground Up; Twenty-First Century Combat as Politics*, Hurst, London, 2012: Frank Ledwidge, *Investment in Blood: The Real Cost of Britain's Afghan War*, Yale University Press, New Haven, 2013; Jack Fairweather, *The Good War: Why We Couldn't Win the War or the Peace in Afghanistan*, Jonathan Cape, London, 2014.
18. See the horrific accounts in Joshua E. S. Phillips, *None of Us were Like this Before: American Soldiers and Torture*, Verso, London, 2010.
19. YouGov Survey, 28–29 August 2013, www.yougov.com
20. 'Public wary of military intervention in Libya: Broad concern that the US is overcommitted', Pew Research Center, 14 March 2011. 'Diminished public appetite for military force—Mideast oil', Pew Research Center, 6 September 2006.
21. Niall Ferguson, 'Carving out Trump's new world order', *Sunday Times*, 20 November 2016.
22. Andrew M. Dorman, *Blair's Successful War: British Military Intervention in Sierra Leone*, Ashgate, Farnham, 2009, pp. 103–125. This is by no means a universal view but it was accepted by the British government see Seuman Milne, *The Revenge of History: The Battle for the Twenty-First Century*, Verso, London, 2012.
23. Dorman, *Successful War*, p. 145. Some other accounts either avoid discussing the British contribution at all or argue that it undervalued the UN's contribution. See Funmi Olonisakin, *Peacekeeping in Sierra Leone: The Story of UNAMISIL*, Lynne Rienner, Boulder, 2008; Emmanuel C. Nwagboso, *Anarchy and the Quest for Political Stability in Sierra Leone*, Edwin Mellen Press, Lampeter, Wales, 2013.
24. Ledwidge, *Investment in Blood*; Mike Clarke, 'The ending of wars and the ending of eras', *RUSI Journal*, August/September 2015, p. 6 May 2013; 'Afghanistan war to cost every household in the UK over £2000', *The Guardian*, 30 May 2013; 'The remnants of a foreign policy', *The Economist*, 11 October 2014, p. 38.
25. Brian Crozier, *The Masters of Power*, Eyre and Spottiswoode, London, 1969, pp. 15–57. Douglas Porch, *The Portuguese Armed Forces and the Revolution*, Croom Helm, London, 1977.
26. Marquis Curzon of Kedleston, *Tales of Travel*, Hodder and Stoughton, London, 1923, p. 52.
27. Arnold Wilson, *Mesopotamia 1917–1920: A Clash of Loyalties*, Oxford University Press, Oxford, 1931; Aylmer Haldane, *The Autobiography of General Sir Aylmer Haldane*, William Blackwood, Edinburgh, 1948; Bertram Thomas, *Alarms and Excursions in Arabia*, George Allen and Unwin, London, 1931, pp. 95–111.
28. Philip Towle, *Pilots and Rebels: The Use of Aircraft in Unconventional Warfare*, Brassey's, London, 1989.

29. Elie Kedourie, 'Arab political memoirs', *Encounter*, November 1972, pp. 70–83.
30. For some of the political complexities in Iraq see Nicholas Krohley, *The Death of the Mehdi Army: The Rise, Fall and Revival of Iraq's most Powerful Militia*, Hurst, London, 2015.
31. Max Hastings, *All Hell Let Loose: The World at War 1939–1945*, Harper/Collins, London, 2012, pp. 464–469.
32. Robert B. Asprey, *War in the Shadows: The Guerrilla in History*, Doubleday, New York, 1975, pp. 478–479.
33. Walter Laqueur, *Guerrilla: A Historical and Critical Study*, Weidenfeld and Nicolson, London, 1977, p. 219.
34. Hastings, *All Hell* pp. 464–69.
35. M. J. Armitage and R. A. Mason, *Airpower in the Nuclear Age 1945–1984*, Macmillan, Basingstoke, 1985, p. 113.
36. IISS, *Military Balance 1974–1975*, London, 1974, pp. 19 and 22.
37. James Sheehan, *The Monopoly of Violence: Why Europeans Hate Going to War*, Faber and Faber, London, 2008.
38. Gallup, November 2014.
39. Gallup, 16 May 2011.
40. Gallup 24 October 2013.
41. President George W. Bush, 'Remarks at West Point: "New threats require new thinking"' in Micah Sifry and Christopher Cerf, *The Iraq War Reader*, Touchstone, New York, 2003, p. 271.
42. Gallup, 14 July 2016 and 1 June 2017.
43. Gallup, 21 November 2012 and 1 June 2017.
44. '162,000 dead: final toll from war is not the end of the story', *The Times*, 3 January 2012.
45. Howard, 'Many Reasons', p. 25.
46. Bass Gary J. *Freedom's Battle: The Origins of Humanitarian Intervention*, Knopf, New York, 2008.
47. See Simon Rogers Editor, *The Hutton Inquiry and Its Impact*, Politico's Guardian Books, London, 2004. *Review of intelligence on Weapons of Mass Destruction: Report of a Committee of Privy Councillors*, chairman Lord Butler, Stationery Office, London, 2014.

CHAPTER 9

# Memory as Guidance

**Abstract** Our decisions are based on our memories and statesmen who lead the nations use history as their guide. Without such knowledge a society would collapse. Other props, such as oracles, which guided the ancients, have been discredited. In their absence we rely either on analogies with past events or on extrapolation from recent trends, yet both are fallible. Booms turn to busts, population expansion to decline, military success to failure. Analogies are useful didactic tools and put current events into perspective but each case is unique and the issue is whether one event has sufficient in common with a past one to make analogy a useful guide. Historians are not immune from mistakes but those historians who say they should not participate in contemporary political debates leave the field open to the less well informed. Above all they need to tell those with power to be cautious because major policy decisions are at best a matter of well-informed guesswork.

**Keywords** Analogy • Extrapolation • Historians • Oracles

It is easy to blame the nations' leaders for the problems described in earlier chapters but everyone consciously or unconsciously relies on extrapolations from recent events or analogies with more distant episodes to guess what will happen to them and to their society. Yet the historians, who are the experts on the past, are often reluctant to predict and, when they do, their predictions are frequently inaccurate.[1] If they were invariably able to foresee the effect of different policies ministers would be surrounded by historical advisers when decisions are being made about foreign intervention to stop civil wars. They are not. Some advisers happen to have been educated as historians but they are not generally recruited because of their training. Nor is this because of popular opposition, on the contrary 'why don't we learn from history?' is a familiar cry when Western governments encounter resistance after involving themselves in foreign disputes. An understanding of history, or rather our memory of history and its limitations is then central to the problem governments have today when dealing with cries of victimisation past and present.

From the moment we are born haphazard memories of our own experiences and later of what we are told about the past determine our attitudes and behaviour.[2] Consciously and mainly unconsciously we work by extrapolating from the past or by analogy hoping that the past gives some idea what a new event is like and how it might best be handled. Just as eyesight connects people and things together in the visible world so memories and only memories can make sense of events. The baby has to learn that objects placed in the air will not stay there unless supported, what things are edible or likeable and what the expressions on faces mean. In old age sufferers from advanced dementia, which destroys the memory, can no longer feed themselves, walk or remember the names and faces of their children; they become more helpless than a year-old child because they can no longer learn from their experiences. A society which lost even a major part of its collective memory would not survive, as indeed happened when the Roman Empire collapsed. Then in Britain and elsewhere cities shrank and technologies such as central heating or road and aqueduct building, were forgotten for hundreds of years.[3] The founder of the Ford motor company, Henry Ford might say that history is more or less bunk but he would not have made a single car without knowledge of previous technical developments.[4]

'History', in the narrow academic sense, is the collection, selection and analysis of the remains, records and memories of a people or group. Dictionaries may define it as 'the continuous methodical record of important or public events' but people and circumstance decide which of the innumerable facts are 'important' enough to recall.[5] Moreover lessons at school, what we have read and what we have seen on film or television determine the tiny aspect of history that is lodged in our memory. Of course that does not mean that facts are all invented as some would have it today; the Holocaust and the moon landing did take place, there was indeed a man called George Washington and Napoleon and Hitler were defeated. But anyone reading past diaries or newspapers will find they contain far more stories than can ever be retold in history books. Whole areas of history, such as women's studies, have been 'discovered' in recent years. At the same time even the most educated people in the West are nearly always less well informed about the ancient Greek and Roman worlds and their languages than their predecessors would have been.[6] In recent years history's focus has moved from the heroes to the victims; during the Renaissance memoirs of those involved in conflict described what they thought were important military and political events without much reference to the victims who were simply dismissed. In the modern age their suffering is a central focus of history although it will be stressed or suppressed to fit in with the culture and political ideas of a particular people.[7] Thus Japanese histories of the 1930s and the Second World War are often very different from their Chinese or Western equivalents because they ignore many of the victims who foreign memoirs and histories consider central.[8]

Modern man has reduced the number of props on which governments can openly rely when making decisions. In the classical world people consulted priests, omens or prophets to provide guidance.[9] According to one account of the most famous example of the process, 'for a thousand years of recorded history the Greeks and Romans, sometimes as private individuals, sometimes as ambassadors, came to Delphi to consult the prophetess. Her words were taken to reveal the will of the gods'.[10] In later centuries religion was a powerful guide and in many cases it is still an important factor though usually in the West it is unadmitted or unconscious. Until the middle of the nineteenth century most international treaties contained references to God to give them greater authority.

Politicians still sometimes rely on astrological forecasts though President Reagan and his wife caused a mixture of ridicule and astonishment when it was found that they were consulting astrologers to decide the timing of international conferences.[11] In South Korea there was a constitutional crisis after the discovery in 2016 that someone, alleged to be a shaman, was influencing President Park Geun-hye's policies.[12] If prayer, oracles and astrology are no longer openly acceptable, extrapolation from what decision makers recall of past events or analogies with them hold sway.[13] But these have some similarities with the oracular method. The oracle at

Delphi bent her prophecies out of fear of tyrants just as modern historians who lived under the dictatorships of Stalin and Mao had to bend their writings or teaching to the dictator's whim.[14] The oracle's prophecies were sometimes enigmatic and so invariably are the 'lessons of history'.

Generals and admirals are often lampooned for preparing for the last war but everyone metaphorically 'prepares for the last war' all the time. In any case extrapolation is not absurd, most processes do continue as they have been doing even in the modern world where changes are far more frequent than they have ever been. As far as the military sphere is concerned, if a type of equipment, such as a warship or tank, failed in the past it may well be outdated and commanders would be open to criticism if they continued to order such apparently obsolete weapons. On the other hand, the equipment might have failed because it was badly maintained, incompetently handled in battle or just unsuitable for the terrain and weather. Those who have developed an attachment to particular weapons, such as cavalrymen in the past, find reasons to explain their recent failures. Governments behave in the same way.

Tony Blair's Chief of Staff, Jonathan Powell explained that the British government joined in the US attack on Iraq in 2003 partly because it believed that Saddam Hussein was developing weapons of mass destruction as he had done previously; 'we had the assumption because Saddam Hussein had lied about using WMD [against Iran and the Kurds] and he had lied about getting rid of them … it would have taken some strong evidence to suggest he had got rid of them.'[15] Altogether Iraq had previously broken or prepared to break three of the international agreements on weapons of mass destruction; the 1925 Geneva Protocol which prohibits the use of chemical and biological weapons, the 1968 nuclear Non-Proliferation Treaty which bans states party to the agreement without nuclear weapons from acquiring them or trying to do so and the 1972 Convention on Biological Weapons which prohibits their production. Saddam Hussein was like a multiple rapist who escapes arrest only to be caught and sentenced for a crime he did not commit.

If extrapolation, or failure to extrapolate, are both fallible strategies depending on circumstances, so are historical analogies partly because, as we see in the next chapter, all the main actors try to 'bend' history to justify their behaviour.[16] Each situation is unique and its particular qualities have to be understood but so do the similarities.[17] Russia has been invaded three times over the last two centuries and each time the invader has been fully aware of the disaster which overtook the previous invaders but has explained it away. Napoleon's aide Count Philippe de Ségur recorded later that during his invasion the French Emperor, 'on comparing [Charles XII of Sweden's 1709] expedition with his own, found a thousand differences between them on which he laid great stress and of what use is the example of the past, in a world where there were never two men, two things or two situations exactly alike?'[18] Conversely, the American and British governments hoped that Saddam Hussein would be unseated by the Iraqi people when they drove his forces out of Kuwait in 1991. They might have recalled that the Greek military junta was overthrown following its failed attempt to unite Cyprus with Greece in 1974 and the Argentine junta was dismissed after its army was unable to hold the Falkland Islands after they captured them in 1982. But Saddam Hussein was not overthrown in 1991, even though his army suffered a more costly defeat including the bombing of his capital during the war over Kuwait than the Greeks or Argentines had done over the conflicts in 1974 and 1982. Moreover, there were risings against him in the south of Iraq and amongst the Kurds while there were no comparable rebellions against the governments which fell in Greece and Argentina. But Saddam Hussein's regime was much more dictatorial than the other two. It had a ferocious police force and armed forces that were delighted to take vengeance on the rebels as compensation for their humiliation at allied hands. Iraqi political culture was far more brutal than Argentine or Greek.

Twelve years later, the US government hoped that the invasion of Iraq itself would finally push the dictator from his position. According to the well-informed journalist, Bob Woodward, the general in charge of the invasion of Iraq in 2003 told President Bush that support for Saddam Hussein's regime would disappear when the US intervened; Woodward commented, 'this important argument was based less on solid intelligence from inside Iraq than assumptions about how people *should* feel towards a ruthless dictator'.[19] But events quickly showed that, while most Kurds and Shiites probably welcomed the invasion at least for a while, many of the minority Sunnis who had ruled Iraq for decades realised that their privileges were now threatened. Iraqis tended to resent the presence of foreign troops and the humiliation of their country and its armed forces at foreign hands. Anti-American rebels made the situation worse because their actions forced the occupiers to isolate themselves in military compounds and to race through the cities in armoured convoys. Many Iraqis opposed any form of control in the swarming cities which had grown up because of the drift from the countryside in recent decades.[20] The fissures in Iraqi opinion were much deeper than the unity provided by the opposition to Saddam Hussein which the allies expected. Great decisions are largely based on intuition or analogies with random memories which can prove to be misleading.

So why not call in the professional historians? Firstly because they are generally more concerned with the way in which they and their colleagues are influenced in their interpretation of the past by current events than about the influence of popular history on present decisions. For politicians and political scientists the reverse is the case.[21] Marxists and other historicists, who claim to have discovered a general theory that will accurately predict the future from the past, have been discredited.[22] Historians traditionally see their job as relating the truth about the past and teaching their students to take an analytical approach to historical material, not to influence current policy or to predict the future.[23] However, after the horrors of the first half of the twentieth century some felt that they and their colleagues could not take a detached view of politics.[24] They were also encouraged by those from other disciplines to participate in current political debates.[25]

Historians sometimes use analogies between historical periods as a didactic tool to bring out the comparisons and contrasts between them, the conditions in which people lived and the problems that faced them. They also suggest that similar situations have some propensity to produce similar results. Lewis Namier, the historian of the eighteenth century, suggested that neighbouring countries tended to confront each other and to form alliances with states on the other side of their potential enemies—the so-called law of odd and even numbers.[26] But plainly this is only a propensity not a universal rule, Mexico and Canada do not usually unite against the United States. Similarly, revolutionary states have often proved much stronger than potential enemies have assumed. They appear chaotic and repressive although they are also highly motivated and militarily effective; examples include Cromwell's England, Napoleon's France, Stalin's Soviet Union or Mao's China.[27] But some revolutionary states are just chaotic and unable to protect themselves against attack; an example is Pol Pot's Cambodia which was easily overrun by the battle-hardened Vietnamese in 1978. In other words history can do no more than suggest tendencies not point to certainties.

Because each situation is unique and their attention is focused on the past historians have not proved invariably prescient when they have participated in topical political debates. They fail to allow for the importance of emotion and the irrational in decision making.[28] Absorbed in history they find it difficult to see how much the world is changing or is going to alter with shocking suddenness.[29] E. H. Carr, subsequently the author of a multi-volume history of the Soviet Union, claimed in 1942, that 'the foundations of liberal democracy and laissez-faire [have] crumbled away' and that small states were out of date. Yet this was the moment when the United States was emerging as a global super power committed to liberalism and capitalism, and when the end of colonialism meant that the world would come to teem with small states some, such as Singapore and Taiwan, highly successful because they are much easier to govern than their larger neighbours.[30] Plainly Carr was just extrapolating from the 1930s when the Great Depression swept over the Western states and when the Axis powers showed a total disregard for the independence of weaker countries. However, until the 1960s Carr's view that communism had proved more successful than capitalism, particularly in the Third World, was widespread amongst historians and other analysts.[31]

In 1963 the Cambridge historian, F. H. Hinsley, later the author of the highly regarded official history of British Intelligence in the Second World War, suggested that distrust between the Soviet Union and the United States would 'certainly be sufficient to prevent the conclusion of agreements on such matters as disarmament and nuclear tests'. That year the Partial Test Ban Treaty was signed by the US and Soviet Union banning nuclear tests in the atmosphere, outer space and under water, and within a decade the first Strategic Arms Limitation agreement was negotiated restricting the numbers of US and Soviet offensive nuclear weapons and anti-ballistic missile systems.[32] Extrapolating from the worst days of the Cold War and drawing analogies with the behaviour of Great Powers in the inter-war years, Hinsley underestimated the extent to which the two potential enemies could find common cause in saving money, reassuring their people and stabilising their relationship to reduce the dangers of nuclear catastrophe.

Hinsley and Carr were not claiming to be familiar with the culture of the various countries about which they were writing but the Cambridge historian, Percival Spear did indeed try to do just that and he proved to be as inaccurate when he tried to foresee their future. He had spent a lifetime studying South Asian culture and history, yet in 1952 he predicted that the newly independent state of Pakistan would adapt more easily to modernisation than India. The larger state was, in his view, more heterogeneous, less individualistic and more divided by the caste system. Hinduism was more otherworldly than Islam while 'little future can be foreseen for scholastic Muslim thought which made of Islam a religion of authority based on a divinely and verbally inspired book literally interpreted'.[33] Clearly Islam has not developed as Spear forecast and those passionately committed to its conservative versions now challenge the great powers as well as weak governments in their home countries. Over the last 60 years India has maintained its democratic institutions while Pakistan broke in half and has lurched from military coup to coup.[34] Pakistanis often regard the production of nuclear weapons as their greatest achievement, Indians see their secular state, democracy and their information technology industry in this light. Hinduism proved more flexible than Spear expected, Islam less and most Muslim countries have found it difficult to establish stable, industrialised states.

Of course there have been other historians whose intuition and use of analogy have proved more prescient. In his Winston Churchill Lecture the military historian, Correlli Barnett drew a comparison between the weakness of the British economy, which helped to bring about the collapse of its empire from 1942 onwards, and the shortcomings of the Soviet economy as he saw them in 1982 and the prospects for its own empire. He correctly forecast the increasing difficulties which Moscow would face though he implied that Marxist ideology would prevent it voluntarily shrinking 'Soviet Russia's role into proportion with her economic base'. Yet this is precisely what Mikhail Gorbachev was to do voluntarily or by mistake after he became General Secretary of the Soviet Communist Party.[35] It was almost as if he had read Barnett's warnings but when he came into office most foreign correspondents and experts on the Soviet Union failed to appreciate that he had understood how policy must change. David Satter of the *Financial Times* commented on Gorbachev's first interview with a Western journal in September 1985, 'when he said that the Soviet Union … did not thirst for American technology, and was trying to break the "vicious circle" of the arms race, he was clearly not telling the truth'.[36] But he was being honest at least about his attitude towards the arms race.

Historians and other commentators rarely predict the election or takeover of a state by an outsider or someone with opinions at odds with previous experience. As in forecasts of Soviet behaviour they expect a state to try to increase its power and influence not to shrink it to fit economic circumstances.[37] Few commentators before 2016 expected the election in the United States of someone like Donald Trump who denounced the alliances and agreements on trade and climate which previous US leaders had spent years or even decades designing and supporting. On the contrary they expected Washington to seek more allies to balance growing Chinese power.[38] Trump was elected in part because his campaign emphasised the contrast between the poverty in many parts of his own country and its expenditure abroad, between the state of its infrastructure and its foreign aid, between its open door to foreign imports and the collapse of its own industries.[39]

It is because even the most distinguished historians and commentators find it hard to see when analogies and extrapolations from the past are misleading that history should be used with caution. But a historian who pretends that policy makers do not have to rely on their memory of history to make their decisions is like an expert on climate who refuses to admit that his or her work has any relevance to current debates about global warming or an expert on anatomy who dismisses the notion that his subject has any relevance to surgery. It is then just an evasion of responsibility for the distinguished historian, G. M. Trevelyan to suggest that 'we never know enough about the infinitely complex circumstances of any past event to prophesy the future by analogy'.[40] We all use past events every moment of our lives to imagine and plan for the future although the task of the statesman is more complex than that of the private individual because he or she has to take untold millions of lives into account. All they can do is to take the best advice and bring as much historical knowledge to the table as possible while being aware that some untoward event may throw out all their careful calculations. This is most particularly the case in foreign policy where understanding of the historical background to a crisis is essential and only too often has been sadly inadequate.

## Notes

1. Michael Howard, *The Lessons of History*, Clarendon Press, Oxford, 1991, chaps 1 and 13.
2. Carl Becker, *Everyman his Own Historian: Essays on History and Politics*, Appleton-Century-Crofts, New York, 1935, pp. 233–255.
3. Though of course there were other technical developments in the Medieval period see Jean Gimpel, *The Medieval Machine: The Industrial Revolution of the Middle Ages*, Gollancz, London, 1996.
4. Interview in *The Chicago Tribune*, 25 May 1916.
5. J. B. Sykes, Editor, *The Concise Oxford English Dictionary*, Clarendon, Oxford, 1986, p. 472.

6. W. A. L. Vincent, *The Grammar Schools: Their Continuing Tradition 1660–1714*, John Murray, London, 1969, pp. 74–81.
7. Yuval Noah Harari, *Renaissance Military Memoirs: War, History and Identity, 1450–1600*, Boydell Press, Woodbridge, 2004. Harari is a lecturer at the Hebrew University in Jerusalem.
8. See Colonel Masanobu Tsuji, *Singapore: The Japanese Version*, Constable, London, 1960; Hyoe Murakami, *Japan: The Years of Trial and Hope: 1919–52*, Kodansha International, Tokyo, 1983; Higashinakano Shudo, *The Nanking Massacre: Fact Versus Fiction*, Sekai Shuppan, Tokyo, 2005.
9. Antony Andrewes, *Greek Society*, Penguin, Harmondsworth, 1971, pp. 266–270.
10. H. W. Parke and D. E. W. Wormell, *The Delphic Oracle*, Basil Blackwell, Oxford, Volume 1, p. 2.
11. Kitty Kelley, *Nancy Reagan: The Unauthorised Biography*, Bantam Press, London, 1991, pp. 325, 435 and 440; James G. Benze, *Nancy Reagan: On the White House Stage*, University Press of Kansas, Lawrence, 2002, pp. 113, 114 and 116; 'The President's Stargazer: Joan Quigley, astrologer to the Reagans died on October 22, aged 87', *The Economist*, 8 November 2014, p. 98.
12. 'Prophets of piffle', *The Economist*, 12 November 2016, p. 57.
13. Operational analysis is basically a more systematic way of analysing data about the past, see Keith R. Tidman, *The Operations Evaluation Group: A History of Naval Operational Analysis*, Naval Institute Press, Annapolis, 1984.
14. Parke and Wormald, *Delphic*, p. 418.
15. '"Assumptions not evidence" led Blair into Iraq War', *The Times*, 19 January 2010.
16. For US failures to understand Vietnamese culture see Jeffrey Race, *War Comes to Long An: Revolutionary Conflict in a Vietnamese Village*, University of California Press, Berkeley, 1972, p. ix. See also Hy V. Luong, *Tradition, Revolution, and Market Economy in a North Vietnamese Village, 1925–2006*, University of Hawai'i Press, Honolulu, 2010.
17. The Israeli-American Nobel Prize winning Psychiatrist, Daniel Kahneman has argued that statistical formulae almost invariably beat intuition in predicting human behaviour and achievement. The problem is that history and international relations so rarely provide usable statistics. See Daniel Kahneman, *Thinking Fast and Slow*, Allen Lane/Penguin, London, 2011, pp. 222–233.
18. General Count Philippe de Ségur, *History of the Expedition to Russia, 1812*, Stroud, 2005, Volume 1, p. 212.
19. Bob Woodward, *Plan of Attack*, Simon and Schuster, London, 2004, p. 81.

20. Nicholas Krohley, *Death of the Medhdi Army: Insurgency and Civil Society in Occupied Baghdad*, Hurst, London, 2014.
21. R. G. Collingwood, *The Idea of History*, Oxford Paperbacks, Oxford University Press, London, 1961; E. H. Carr, *What is History?* Penguin, Harmondsworth, 1964. For classic examples of the examination of this two- way process see H. Butterfield, *Christianity and History*, G. Bell, London, 1949 and Marc Bloch, *The Historian's Craft*, Manchester University Press, Manchester, 1992.
22. Karl R. Popper, *The Poverty of Historicism*, Routledge, Kegan, Paul, London, 1957; See also Richard Pares' refutation of Arnold Toynbee's *Study of History* in Richard Pares, *The Historian's Business and Other Essays*, Clarendon, Oxford, 1961, pp. 11-33.
23. G. R. Elton, *Return to Essentials: Some Reflections on the Present State of Historical Study*, Cambridge University Press, Cambridge 1991.
24. Geoffrey Barraclough, *History in a Changing World*, Oxford University Press, 1955, p. 7. See also the debates about the work of the Australian historian, Geoffrey Blainey in Stuart Macintyre and Anna Clark, *The History Wars*, Melbourne University Press, Melbourne, 2004.
25. Colin Clark, 'The "Golden Age" of the Great Economists: Keynes, Robbins et al. in 1930', *Encounter*, June 1977, p. 86. See also the blistering attack on Tawney in Elton, *Return*, p. 86. Elton claimed there was not a word of Tawney's writings which could be relied upon.
26. Sir Newis Namier, *Vanished Supremacies*, Penguin, Harmondsworth, 1962, p. 209.
27. Jonathan R. Adelman, *Revolution, Armies and War: A Political History*, Lynne Rienner, Boulder, CO, 1985. Adelman is a professor at the University of Denver.
28. Bruce Catton, *Prefaces to History*, Doubleday, New York, 1970, p. 64.
29. E. H. Carr, *Conditions of Peace*, Macmillan, London, 1942, pp. 106 and 66. F. H. Hinsley, *Power and the Pursuit of Peace: Theory and Practice in the History of International Relations between States*, Cambridge University Press, Cambridge, 1963. Percival Spear, *India, Pakistan and the West*, Oxford University Press, London, 1952. Correlli Barnett, 'The Soviet Empire and the British Empire: A Strategic Comparison', *Schweizer Monatshefte*, 62, 1982.
30. Carr, *Conditions*, pp. 66 and 106.
31. Barraclough, *Introduction* pp. 221-224.
32. Hinsley, *Power*, p. 355.
33. Spear, *India, Pakistan*, p. 234. 'NDTV poll: icons from Mahatma Gandhi to Sachin', *The Hindu*, 12 August 2007.
34. This is not however how Pakistanis see the comparison. According to a poll published in 2016 86 % of Pakistanis believe their system of government is

democratic, 42 % believe that China is fully democratic and 26 % believe the same of India, 'Political parties, democracy, climate change', Gilani Research Foundation, 25 March 2016.
35. Correlli Barnett, 'The Soviet Empire and the British Empire'.
36. David Satter, 'The Foreign Correspondent: On Manipulation and Self-Deception', *Encounter*, May 1987, p. 59. Satter went on to write several books on the Soviet Union and Russia.
37. See Paul Kennedy's classic study, *The Rise and Fall of the Great Powers*, Unwin/Hyman, London, 1988.
38. Brendan Taylor and William T. Tow, 'Conclusion' in Joanne Wallis and Andrew Carr, Editors, *Asia-Pacific Security: An Introduction*, Georgetown University Press, Washington, 2016, pp. 264–265.
39. For a vivid personal description of the poverty, backwardness and anger see J. D. Vance, *Hillbilly Elegy*, HarperCollins, New York, 2016.
40. G. M. Trevelyan, *An Autobiography and Other Essays*, Longmans, Green, London, 1949, p. 84.

CHAPTER 10

# Hiding Victimisation

**Abstract** Although governments and other institutions rely on past experience to guide them they know that all history is shaped by the participants and they try to shape it themselves. Totalitarian governments try for years afterwards to hide their horrific crimes by lies and repression. But democratic politicians also lie and obfuscate when faced with intensive questions from the media. However, if they acquire a reputation for mendacity the public will quickly turn against them. In wartime they censor the media often with enthusiastic public support and they sometimes do the same in a time of general peace when publication of particular facts may lead to violence between communities. If historians can eventually show what 'really happened' they have to follow a tortuous road.

**Keywords** Censorship • Lies • Massacres • Reputation

Most institutions and influential people are tempted to 'bend' or control history as it unfolds so that they are not lodged in people's memory as victimisers.[1] Whether they are companies, political parties, Churches, voluntary social organisations or states they all have the same instinct. Even if their members compete and argue bitterly amongst themselves they tend to defend their profession or institution against outside criticism. Totalitarian and dictatorial governments have by far the most victims to hide but every institution tries to justify itself and to minimise general knowledge of its mistakes and misdemeanours. Sympathisers with a particular institution tend to go along with this process because they push them out of their memory and regard examples of victimisation as random and unfortunate rather than intrinsic to its culture and ideology.

Amongst totalitarian governments historical distortions are the tribute that vice pays to virtue. In 1943, at the height of the Second World War, the Nazis announced the discovery of the bodies of some 4000 Polish officers murdered in March 1940. The Germans and Soviets had invaded Poland the year before and divided it between them. Acting under orders from Stalin and his entourage the Soviets had murdered altogether some 14,000 Poles because they came from the upper classes and were likely to be irreconcilable to their rule. By 1943 the Germans were in the midst of their policy of obliterating the Jews of Europe principally by gassing them. They were also murdering gypsies and communists and Soviet prisoners of war who were too weak to slave in their factories.[2] Their policy was brutal beyond all imagining. But so was the Soviet. In the 1920s and 1930s the Bolshevik regime had killed between 12 and 20 million of its own people. The communists usually chose starvation as their favoured method of general massacre, an ironic perversion given that Marxist governments were supposed to raise the standards of living of the poor.[3] Nazi and Communist governments were as close to absolute evil as it is possible for a government to become.

Both knew that their standards and behaviour would be shocking to most people who were not unbalanced by their emotions. Hitler and his colleagues tried to cover up the mass murders they had committed in the concentration camps as their forces retreated towards the end of the war and some of their sympathisers have continued to this day to deny the reality of the Holocaust. Communists and ex-communists have only reluctantly admitted their crimes. So it was not moral outrage which led the Nazis to reveal the Katyn murders in 1943 but to make mischief between the allies. And, to an extent, they succeeded at least between the Polish government in exile in London and the Soviet regime. The Poles fell into the trap by asking for a neutral investigation to establish what had happened to their officers. No doubt they felt outraged and sickened by the cold-blooded murder of their friends and relations. Perhaps they also believed it would be easier to establish the truth then than after the end of the war. But, shortly afterwards, the Soviets denounced the Polish government and said that they would only recognise the so-called Lublin government of communist Poles. The breach between the London Poles and Moscow would probably have happened anyway. Stalin wanted to move Russia's frontiers westwards into what had been Polish territory before the war and to hand vast swathes of historic Germany to the Poles. The Polish government would have rejected this and it appears to have been one of the motives for the Katyn murders. Thousands of the relatives of the Polish officers killed were sent off to Kazakhstan so that the area could be ethnically cleansed.[4]

The Nazi revelations also presented the British and American governments with a dilemma. They knew, or suspected, that the Soviets were responsible for the murder of the officers. They were aware that Stalin and Hitler were both mass murderers, though they did not know how many they had killed. But they had to bend every effort to win the war. And they and their publics were aware that the Soviet army was doing most of the fighting and Nazi-killing in Europe. Half the British answering one poll in April 1943 felt the Soviets were doing more to win the war than any of the other allied nations.[5] So governments had to hide their suspicions and this was easier for them because they and their publics were not emotionally involved in the way that the Poles were. It was not until after the war that US investigators proved the Soviets were responsible for the massacre and by then this had become an esoteric piece of history not easily lodged in the public memory.[6] It was not until the Gorbachev era that the Soviets finally admitted their crime and released the papers demonstrating that Stalin himself had signed the instructions ordering the massacre.[7] This might never have come to light even under Gorbachev if the exiled Poles had not struggled for decades to have the massacre remembered and investigated. After all it was only one mass crime amongst the myriad of others the totalitarians committed; there are few memorials in the West for the gypsies, Poles and other East Europeans killed by the Nazis. Few outside those regions remember the Kazakhs, Ukrainians and others starved to death by Stalin.[8]

As far as Stalin's purges were concerned, it was not until 1956 that Khrushchev admitted some of these to delegates at the twentieth Party Congress and even then he did not deplore the 'liquidation' of the 'exploiting classes' but only the destruction of the supporters of Zinoviev and other communist intellectuals. He said that confessions were forced out of such people and that Stalin acted through 'administrative violence, mass repressions, and terror' against thousands of people. Of the 139 candidates who were elected to the XVII Party Central Committee in 1934, 98 were arrested and shot; of the 1966 delegates to the same Congress, 1108 were arrested on charges of anti-revolutionary crimes.[9]

In time the speech was leaked to the West, translated and widely publicised. Of course there were ardent communists and sympathisers abroad who never believed the allegations or dismissed them because they regarded them as random rather than inherent in the ideology and because they disliked their own society and particularly the United States. Writing in 1973 Paul Hollander of Harvard University traced the pilgrimages that communist sympathisers had made first to the Soviet Union, then to China, Albania and North Vietnam. 'All of these countries' he noted, 'tend to be viewed at the time of the visit as victims—victims of history, of backwardness, and (more importantly) of the West'.[10]

What is clear is that communists have been far more successful than Nazis at hiding their own victims or excusing their actions to give them a relatively favourable image.[11] While both were demonic there are still Western defenders of communism and intellectuals had no shame in admitting that they once gave it their support. Writers like Jean Paul Sartre continued to be treated with respect long after Stalin's murders were exposed. Communist spies such as Kim Philby had their memoirs published in the West justifying their work for the Soviet Union. The respected novelist, Graham Greene could write in the introduction, the book 'is an honest one, well-written, often amusing ... he "betrayed his country"— yes, perhaps he did, but who among us has not committed treason to something or someone more important than a country?'[12] Greene made a false distinction between a country and the people who live there and Philby betrayed them for a monstrous regime which killed millions of harmless Ukrainians, Kazakhs and Russians. Moreover, Philby did not 'just' betray Britain but, most immediately, his colleagues working for MI6 who he exposed to certain death in the communist world.[13] Efforts to defend Hitler on the grounds that he improved the German roads, reduced unemployment and sponsored the VW car would rightly be regarded with derision and horror, while Stalin is sometimes complimented for industrialising his country and leading it to victory in 1945. Of course, some of this can be put down to the fact that there were far more intellectuals with communist than with Nazi sympathies in the 1930s and to the way that the Nazis were defeated in the Second World War and some of their crimes exposed at the Nuremberg trials. It may be also that it is easier to overlook communist crimes because starvation is less shocking than shooting or gassing people. Famished people die slowly and the perpetrators may be far away from the victims. They can pretend to themselves that the victims' fate has nothing to do with them. But communism's crimes have been revealed to all who want to listen and its economic pretensions shattered.

Yet Russian attitudes to communism are ambiguous. In the decade after the millennium both Britons and Russians were asked to vote in televised contests for those who they regarded as their 'greatest' countrymen. The term was not defined and one can only presume that the people who voted did so for those whom they admired. In 2008 Russian people voted Stalin and Lenin amongst the 'greatest' Russians.[14] It is true that the two communist leaders did have a massive impact on modern Russian history and thus qualify as 'great' in the sense which is often used by historians.[15] But it is possible that the younger generation have never learnt about or have forgotten or forgiven the murders carried out by Stalin and other communists. Over 40 % of Russians in one 2003 poll said they believed the communists' violent seizure of power in 1917 from the moderate Kerensky government was legitimate against only 18 % who believed that the peaceful dissolution of the USSR was legitimate and only 17 % who supported the privatisation of state property in the 1990s. Russians also feel victimised by the West, some 66 % said they agreed with the idea that Russia 'always evoked hostile feelings in other states and none of them wishes Russia well' and a similar proportion believed Western accusations of violation of human rights in Russia were made to discredit Russia rather than concern for Russian citizens.[16]

If democratic politicians cannot hide their victims as effectively as those in autocratic states can do, they want to knead the dough of history as it unfolds so that they can win elections and convince historians of their achievements or justify their decisions. Indeed, John Mearsheimer of the University of Chicago has argued that democratic politicians lie more frequently than dictators not least because they are questioned daily by a hostile media.[17] Chris Woods' study of the use that the US government has made of drone aircraft over recent years suggests that spokesmen have, for example, been tempted to minimise the civilian casualties that have been incurred.[18]

Democratic statesmen caught out lying about their responsibility for disasters generally lose their credibility. Anthony Eden's reputation was ruined by his government's plots and lies over the Suez crisis. The Indian leader, Jawaharlal Nehru dismissed Eden's Foreign Secretary, Selwyn Lloyd as 'intellectually unreliable and morally dishonest'.[19] President

Eisenhower claimed that his own greatest asset was his reputation for honesty but, when a US reconnaissance aircraft was shot down over the Soviet Union, his administration foolishly denied that the aircraft had been authorised to spy on the Soviets. Eisenhower could have claimed that he had a right to send U2s over the Soviet Union given that Soviet satellites orbited the United States but, in the event, it was his own reputation which was dented.[20] Richard Nixon's denial of his administration's involvement in the bugging of the Watergate Hotel prevented him being seen as a great statesman even though he and Henry Kissinger ended the US confrontation with China, brought US involvement in Vietnam to an end and negotiated the first major nuclear arms control agreements with the Soviet Union. Any one of these achievements would have been regarded by other presidents as perhaps the most significant triumph in their period in office.[21]

There were, of course victims of the ending of the Vietnam War. The CIA agent, Frank Snepp published a critique of US efforts to hide their abandonment of many of their Vietnamese agents when South Vietnam collapsed in 1975. Admittedly the US Navy managed to fly some out of their embassy compound in the last hours before the North Vietnamese conquest of Saigon but the new rulers sent some 200,000 US sympathisers to re-education camps where they were kept on a starvation diet and forced to clear mines and do other dangerous jobs. Snepp concluded, 'in terms of squandered lives, blown secrets and the betrayal of friends and collaborators, our handling of the evacuation was an institutional disgrace'.[22] According to his account, officials tried to prevent Snepp writing a book on the subject and, when this failed, to force him to hand over any profits.

In 2013 Eric Schlosser published a dramatic study of American accidents involving nuclear weapons during the Cold War years which showed how nearly these caused widespread casualties.[23] According to this account, there were several such events. B52 bombers carrying nuclear weapons crashed in Spain, Canada, Britain and the United States. A Titan missile exploded in the United States scattering nuclear debris. Official comments on these incidents at the time hid the dangers of nuclear explosions or contamination. Something had been known or guessed but now the extent of the dangers was only too clear. One can but speculate about what would have happened had the truth not been hidden. It seems likely that the B52s would have been deprived of their nuclear role much earlier, indeed public opinion in the US might have insisted that the country rely on nuclear submarines rather than land-based systems. There would also have been greater pressure to reduce the thousands of nuclear weapons that had been produced. The arms control agreements between West and East moved far in this direction after the end of the Cold War but they might have been given an extra and earlier push by a better-informed and alarmed public.

In a world war the pressure to hide the truth about disasters is much stronger than in peacetime. Churchill hid his responsibility for many of the victims of his strategy during the Second World War such as the abortive Norwegian campaign in 1940 and the disaster at Singapore some months later.[24] Singapore was particularly important because its capture by the Japanese in February 1942 undermined the whole allied position in Southeast Asia, left thousands of Commonwealth soldiers and millions of Asians at the mercy of the Japanese army which had been brutalised by its education, training and its years of anti-guerrilla operations in China. Yet there was no official investigation of this most far-reaching British disaster. The American naval analyst George Melton has argued with some justification that Churchill's decision to destroy the French fleet in 1940 was both unnecessary because the French admirals were determined not to let it fall into Nazi hands and counterproductive because it killed over a thousand French sailors, alienated the mass of French people and failed to destroy most of the ships. However, Churchill presented it as a necessary 'victory' because it ensured that the US government would believe the British would continue to fight against the Nazis.[25]

More generally, democratic societies have to wrestle with the fact that publicity can cost lives; should free speech or suffering be prioritised? In 1997 Louisa Burns-Bisogno, an American television writer and lecturer published *Censoring Irish Nationalism* a comprehensive critique of British, American and Irish governments for censoring films about the IRA and Irish nationalism.[26] From her point of view the governments had foiled the creative instincts of the directors, and hidden or distorted the truth about the IRA and the Irish nationalists in general. The subject of Irish nationalism was often studiously ignored by film makers because of government censorship or the qualms of the film companies. Even when it was the subject of film and later of television programmes, nationalist activists were often presented as morally ambiguous figures and the justice of the cause unexplained. Ms Burns-Bisogno makes her position clear as a sympathiser with Irish Republican Army. But, during the period she covers, all three governments were aware that divisions between various nationalists had torn Ireland apart in the civil war which followed independence. In the 1970s the Provisional IRA was to instigate the 'troubles' in Northern Ireland which led to another 3000 deaths. The various governments had to weigh the advantages of leaving film and television directors total freedom against the dangers of further bloodshed. In any case her quotations show that many of the film makers concerned were fully aware of the dangers of fuelling further nationalistic conflicts and carefully chose their material, self-censorship which she describes as insidious. One company which refused to release a film commented, 'our decision is not a matter of commerce, it is a question of civic responsibility to the public and society in which we live.'[27]

Ms Burns-Bisogno's position is the opposite to the one set out in *The Media and the Path to Peace* by the Israeli academic, Gadi Wolfsfeld. He argues that one reason why Northern Ireland has eventually found such a path is that the news media there have sometimes to appeal to both sides. Thus, towards the end of the peace process they tried to avoid stirring up trouble, emphasising divisions and over-dramatising news. Indeed, to the chagrin of partisans, they avoided covering some demonstrations altogether. The peace process was also fortified because a large section of the political elite wanted to end the bloodshed and accepted the limitations in journalistic coverage. In contrast, in Israel the political elite was much more divided over the Oslo Peace Process; Palestinians and Israelis had totally separate media which, as far as the Hebrew press was concerned, showed no restraint in its coverage of disturbances and focused on those on the Palestinian side who favoured violence. In Wolfsfeld's view, 'while there is no reason to expect journalists to support any particular peace initiative, they are obliged to do what they can to lower the risk of violence and war'.[28] Whether or not one accepts this argument or interpretation of the facts it is clear that Dr Wolfsfeld will have been only too familiar with what national conflict means in a situation like Israel's with death, the threat of death and militarisation all around. He contrasts the interviews he carried out with Northern Irish journalists who had seen the effects of terrorism and lost school friends in the conflict with those who pontificated from a safe distance.[29]

Ms Burns-Bisogno did not address this dilemma directly and assumed that government censorship and self-censorship were wrong. However, most people would feel that censorship is sometimes justified; in wartime they would not want to sacrifice their soldiers' lives by revealing military secrets or demoralising people by emphasising their failings. In 1942

American citizens were asked whether the government should give them more information about the fighting if care were taken that this did not help the enemy. Even with the caveat, over 60 % answered in the negative. In one such poll in April of that year 20 % said censorship was not strict enough, 60 % said it was about right and 8 % said it was too strict.[30] Plainly Americans prioritised victory and the saving of US lives in that case over the instincts of editors and their own interest in what was happening. Indeed, many would have regarded too much publicity as close to treason. There is, of course, a fundamental distinction between hiding a fact that could help the enemy and trying to circumscribe journalists' right to express their opinions. Democracies often accept that they will have to put up with the second at least in wars which do not threaten their survival. Thus, critics of a particular war normally have free rein even though their views may encourage the enemy to resist; mass demonstrations in the US against the Vietnam War are a notable example.[31] There is a necessary tension in a democracy, even in a total war, between the belief that the media should improve public morale and the need for constructive criticism of the government.

Given the way in which events are hidden, partially hidden or distorted by governments and by media selection of the news, our understanding of 'history' is bent as it is 'made'. Yet, as pointed out previously it has to be the major guide to those very same institutions. It is rather like washing one's hands in a corner of a basin full of dirty water in the hope that one corner is clean. All the more important that governments should proceed cautiously whether in domestic or foreign policy when more victims may be created and try to avoid irreversible decisions based only on analogies with a limited number of recent events.

## Notes

1. An exception in the modern world was the 'Islamic State' which ruled over parts of Syria and Iraq in 2015 and 2016. It boasted of its atrocities and displayed them on the media to terrorise people. It delighted in its ability to shock the liberal West.
2. Ulrich Herbert, *Hitler's Foreign Workers: Enforced Foreign Labour in Germany under the Third Reich*, Cambridge University Press, Cambridge, 1997.
3. See, for example, Eugenia Ginzburg, *Within the Whirlwind*, Collins/Harvill, London, 1981 and Mukhamet Shayakhmetov, *The Silent Steppe: The Memoir of a Kazakh Nomad under Stalin*, Rookery, New York, 2006.

For general Soviet policy, see Robert Conquest, *The Great Terror: Stalin's Purges of the 1930s*, Penguin, Harmondsworth, 1971 and Alexander Solzhenitsyn. *The Gulag Archipelago: 1918–1956*, Collins/Fontana, London, 1974.

4. Anna M. Cienciala, Natalia S. Lebedeva and Wojciech Materski, *Katyn: A Crime Without Punishment*, Yale University Press, New Haven, 2007, pp. 137–138.
5. Hadley Cantril and Mildred Strunk, *Public Opinion 1935–1946*, Princeton University Press, Princeton, 1951, pp. 1062, 1063, 1065.
6. Stefan Korboniski, *Warsaw in Exile*, George Allen and Unwin, London, 1966, pp. 77–86.
7. 'Katyn killings cast a long shadow on tour', *The Times*, 4 July 1988; Bernard Levin, 'Stalin's authorised massacre', *The Times*, 13 April 1993.
8. Fortunately, a monument was set up in Washington in 2015 to the murdered Ukrainians.
9. N. Khrushchev, *Khrushchev Remembers*, Andre Deutsch, London, 1971. 'Khrushchev's Secret Speech', Appendix 4, p. 572.
10. Paul Hollander, 'The Ideological Pilgrim', *Encounter*, November 1973, pp. 3–15; David Caute, *The Fellow Travellers: Intellectual Friends of Communism*, Yale University Press, New Haven, 1988.
11. In fact there is evidence that Hitler was encouraged in his genocidal ambitions by his interpretation of Marx and Engels and by Soviet example, see George Watson, 'Race and the Socialists', *Encounter*, November 1976, pp. 15–23 and 'Was Hitler a Marxist?', *Encounter*, December 1984, pp. 19–25.
12. Kim Philby, *My Silent War*, Granada, London, 1969, p. 7. See also George Blake, *No Other Choice: An Autobiography*, Jonathan Cape, London, 1990.
13. He also killed those Soviet citizens who wanted to help the West, see Christopher Andrew and Oleg Gordievski, *KGB: The Inside Story*, Hodder and Stoughton, London, 1990, p. 321.
14. Five out of the top six were authoritarian monarchs or dictators, and Stalin was only defeated by about 5500 votes; 'At last, Stalin is defeated by voters', *The Times*, 29 December 2008. The Soviet Union and India were linked diplomatically during the Cold War but India's culture could hardly be a greater contrast, Indians regard Mahatma Gandhi and Mother Teresa as their icons. See 'NDTV poll: icons from Mahatma Gandhi to Sachin', *The Hindu*, 12 August 2007.
15. Simon Sebag Montefiori, 'Is the greatest Russian Stalin or Nicholas? The answer in obvious', *The Times*, 18 July 2008.
16. Yitzhak M. Brudny, 'Myths and national identity in post-communist Russia' in Gerard Bouchard Editor, *National Myths: Constructed Pasts, Contested Presents*, Routledge, London, 2013, pp. 148–151. See also

'NATO publics blame Russia for Ukrainian Crisis, but reluctant to provide military aid', pp. 8–9, Pew Research Center, 10 June 2015.
17. John Mearsheimer, *Why Leaders Lie: The Truth about Lying in International Politics*, Duckworth Overlook, London, 2011, pp. 71–72.
18. Chris Woods, *Sudden Justice: America's Secret Drone Wars*, Hurst, London, 2015, chaps 11 and 12.
19. Philip Ziegler, *Mountbatten: The Official Biography*, Fontana/Collins, London, 1986, p. 556.
20. Stephen Ambrose, *Eisenhower: The President*, George Allen and Unwin, London, 1984, pp. 574–575.
21. Richard Nixon, *The Memoirs of Richard Nixon*, Sidgwick and Jackson, London, 1978.
22. Frank Snepp, *Decent Interval: The American Debacle in Vietnam and the Fall of Saigon*, Penguin, Harmondsworth, 1980, p. 474.
23. Eric Schlosser, *Command and Control*, Penguin, London, 2014.
24. Graham Rhys-Jones, *Churchill and the Norway Campaign*, Pen and Sword, Barnsley, 2008. Ivan Simson, *Singapore: Too Little too Late*, Leo Cooper, London, 1970; Major-General S. Woodburn Kirby, *Singapore: The Chain of Disaster*, Cassell, London, 1970; Clifford Kinvig, *Scapegoat; General Percival of Singapore*, Brasseys, London, 1996.
25. George E. Melton, *From Versailles to Mers el-Kebir*, Naval Institute Press, Annapolis, 2015. For Churchill's version see Winston Churchill, *The Second World War: Volume 11, Their Finest Hour*, Reprint Society, London, 1951, pp. 194–202.
26. Louisa Burns-Bisogno, *Censoring Irish Nationalism: The British, Irish and American Suppression of Republican Images in Film and Television 1905–1995*, McFarland, Jefferson, North Carolina, 1997.
27. Burns-Bisogno, *Censoring Irish Nationalism*, p. 125.
28. Wolfsfeld, *Media*, p. 227.
29. Wolfsfeld, *Media*, p. 180.
30. Cantril, *Public Opinion*, p. 1131.
31. See the contemporary defence of the right to demonstrate by Hans Morgenthau in Hans J. Morgenthau, *Truth and Power: Essays of a Decade 1960–70*, Pall Mall Press, London, 1970, pp. 45–50, 409.

CHAPTER 11

# 2016: The Victory of Victimhood

**Abstract** In 2016 claims of victimhood became for the first time ubiquitous amongst the Great Powers, China, Russia and the United States. Dissatisfied leaders from the Nazis onwards have used such claims to justify their plans to change the status quo. Russia's government argues that NATO and EU interference in its vital interests justify its seizure of Crimea and interventions in Georgia and Ukraine. Russian people support President Putin's policies partly because they feel humiliated by historic events and most recently by the collapse of the Soviet Union. China's government continues to make capital out of Japanese repression in the Second World War to justify its assertive foreign policy and hide its own crimes. The current US administration argues that Washington's past generosity has led it into unfair trade treaties and to 'free-riding' by its NATO allies. Resentment about past events may be justified in some cases but deployed as a weapon by powerful states it is a threat to international stability.

**Keywords** CSCE • Frontiers • Islands • Trump • Ukraine

In 2016 the world-wide emphasis on victimhood reached a new peak when the Republican presidential candidate won the United States' election while claiming that his country was not just the victim of a specific

© The Author(s) 2018
P. Towle, *History, Empathy and Conflict*,
https://doi.org/10.1007/978-3-319-77959-1_11

event, such as the attack on Pearl Harbor or 9/11, but the victim of the prevailing international system. The Russians and Chinese governments had long made a habit of spreading such general claims about their countries' suffering but now the Americans joined the unhappy band. All three governments were trying to lodge their version of past events and the current situation in the national memory and also amongst foreigners. All three accounts were based on a careful selection of the facts to make their case.

Empathy for victims at home and abroad is to be welcomed and is one of the many benefits from the spread of knowledge through education and the media. It has contributed to the long peace between developed countries from 1945 since it helps to keep alive the horrors of the two World Wars. This is like swimming against the current because people become bored with normality and excited by conflict and change. It was after one of the longest periods of general peace that many Europeans and particularly the young and the intellectuals welcomed the outbreak of war in 1914.[1] People crave excitement, which is not fully satisfied by sporting and other harmless ways of sublimating enthusiasms and expending energies. The media advocate the rule of reason but feed on conflict even if they deplore its effects. Their news is predominantly bad news. Good news of the negotiation of treaties, economic and technical development is dull.

Yet our ancestors would be dumfounded to learn that powerful states now stressed their victimhood rather than their power and success. Before the politicisation of the mass of people through education and the media it was assumed that a nation would boast about its military victories and forget its defeats, that successes should be followed by parades and celebrations and that victorious generals should be national figures with statues and other tributes to their successes. Now such parades have generally been replaced in the West by mourning for the casualties. Because this revolution in sensibility has crept up on us over recent decades it is not generally noticed but, when used to demonise other groups, it is as dangerous as the 'frantic boasts and foolish words' of the past. Moreover, it is not likely to change again quickly because politicians find claims of victimisation so useful to arouse public passions.

The winner of the US presidential election in 2016, Donald Trump set out to meet the craving for novelty and sympathy by producing successive stories for the media however surprising and outrageous. He attacked the traditional media for spreading false news while, before he became president, he spread bogus claims that Barack Obama had been born outside the United States and so could not be president. Immediately after taking office he claimed that the crowds celebrating his inauguration were greater than his predecessors' when photographs showed this was false. During his presidency he continued spreading confusion about what was and what was not factually accurate. Trump had worked in television for many years and so he and his circle were more familiar with what excited and interested people than any of his predecessors had been. He saw that 'twitter' was the new way to communicate especially with the young and that many Americans were bored or dissatisfied with politics as normal. White Americans were, he suggested, the victims of Mexicans who had entered the country illegally. Americans had been raped, murdered and robbed by them. Muslims had come into the United States to kill and terrorise people and their entry should be halted or curtailed. Americans had lost their jobs not only because of immigration but of the over-generous trade treaties his predecessors had negotiated. He would denounce these agreements and force US companies manufacturing abroad to bring factories back to the United States. America's allies had victimised the US by depending on it for their protection ever since the Second World War. They should either spend much more on their own defence or the US would cease to support them. All these plaints appealed because poorer Americans could explain their personal difficulties by the failure of the Washington elite to look after their interests. Trump's victory illustrated the power of such appeals to represent foreigners as the victimisers and previous administrations as incompetent or indifferent to the mass of white Americans. Combined with his attention-catching tweets this proved an election winning tactic.

For several decades there had been respected voices warning of the contrast between the shortcomings of the US educational system, health and social care and its burdensome international role. In some respects the US was beginning to look like Britain and the Soviet Union in their declining years. The problem, as the British historian Paul Kennedy pointed out, was that the US political system prevented realistic attempts to respond to the problems. It was in the United States alone of the developed Western nations that the age of death was falling and yet the country spent more on health care than most, as it did on education.[2] Kennedy reminded his readers that tests showed one in seven Americans could not locate their own country on a world map and the majority did not know what the Reformation was. But it was more effective in electoral terms for Donald Trump to portray previous administrations and foreign allies as the victimisers than to admit that there were flaws in the US Constitution or indeed that its laissez-faire ideology was not working to the advantage of the majority. Yet together these prevented reforms so that funds could be allocated more effectively.

Kennedy drew the parallel with Britain and Russia which had both decided that they could not go on maintaining their empires because of the contrast between their declining economies and their imperial pretentions. He suggested that this was the situation in which the United States found itself and that Washington was faced with fundamental choices between radical reform and steady decline. What was contradictory about Donald Trump's position was that he wanted 'to make America great again' while, at the same time, his actions and comments weakened the alliances on which the US would increasingly have to depend if it were to balance its military and social spending.[3] His reforms were radical but they were generally the wrong ones.

The perspectives advanced by Trump's critics were much less worrying to the US elite and the country's allies because they promised more of the same and stressed the advantages of the current international system. The United States had helped found and largely guided almost all the major international and multinational institutions including the United Nations, the World Bank, NATO and the International Monetary Fund. Their country had indeed carried much of the burden for Western defences but he who pays the boatman gets to choose the course. US influence in NATO and amongst its East Asian allies had been predominant. It was, for example, the United States that had led the push for NATO's expansion into Eastern Europe in the 1990s that had so alienated Moscow. It was the United States that had dominated negotiations with the Soviet Union during the tense Cold War years and appointed NATO's senior commanders. If China, Mexico and other countries had benefited from past US trading policies so had the United States. By permitting foreign exports to the United States, Washington had helped its citizens to cheap foreign goods and enabled millions around the world to escape from poverty. In turn the newly enriched masses came to the United States as tourists or students and bought US goods. Trade was beneficial to all in the long run or so the optimists argued. The United States was not the victim of the world outside its borders but the guide to a liberal international system which had, to the extent possible, replaced the dangerous international competition of the past.[4]

After the 2008 financial crisis and the suffering and uncertainty it created Trump recognised that American voters were much more likely to respond to claims that the US was a victim than to appeals to pride in the role the US had played in the world since 1945. He also saw how effective the cry of victimisation was in Russia and China at uniting their people behind the government. Having control of their media and thus to some extent of the national memory authoritarian governments used such complaints as justification for their growing military strength and assertive foreign policy. They staged ceremonies in which their ballistic missiles were dragged through the centre of Moscow or Beijing, something unimaginable in London, Paris or Tel Aviv where governments hid their nuclear power as much as possible.[5] Military strength is often feared and nuclear weapons in particular. Three of the four least favoured countries in the 2014 BBC World Service poll—North Korea, Israel and Pakistan—had nuclear forces and the fourth, Iran was widely suspected by Western intelligence services of trying to develop such weapons at that time.[6] But Presidents Xi and Putin felt confident that their control over their national media, the nationalism of their people and their narratives of victimisation meant that they were as pleased rather than alarmed by the sight of nuclear weapons as they were by their leaders' assertive foreign policies.

Russia has frequently been invaded from the West and its territories laid waste but it was Russian forces which first defeated Napoleon's army in 1812 and tore the heart out of the genocidal Nazi hordes 130 years later. Opinion polls showed that this was understood in Britain and the US in the later stages of the Second World War. They might have won the war without Soviet help but it would have taken years longer not least because of the difficulty of staging an opposed amphibious landing in the face of the highly professional Nazi army. The war would probably have ended as a race to develop and use nuclear weapons which would have left parts of central Europe and perhaps Britain a nuclear wasteland. Yet, however vital their past role for world peace, Russians continued to feel victimised and despised by the West even at the height of their power and influence during the Cold War.[7] These feelings were greatly increased when the Soviet Union collapsed, many of its outlying territories asserted their independence and Moscow had to appeal for Western financial and technical assistance to make safe its decaying nuclear weapons and submarines. From being citizens of one of the two Superpowers Russians suddenly became members of a middle power with a national product only slightly more than half the size of a reunited Germany.[8] It was not until oil and gas exports brought wealth that Moscow began to assert its power effectively in its former territories. In August 2008 Russian forces intervened on behalf of the South Ossetians who had been trying to break away from the new state of Georgia. In March 2014 Russia seized Crimea from Ukraine, incorporated it in its own territories and intervened in the incipient civil war in eastern Ukraine.

Yet Moscow's highest priority at the Conference on Security and Cooperation in Europe (CSCE) which met from the 1973 to 1975 had been international acceptance of the continent's existing borders.[9] Other countries including the Federal Republic of Germany, Ireland and Spain wanted agreement that borders would not be frozen forever and could be changed peacefully. Article 1 (iii) of the Conference's Final Act in 1975 allowed for this but laid down 'the participating states regard as inviolable all one another's frontiers as well as the frontiers of all states in Europe and therefore they will refrain now and in the future from assaulting these frontiers.'[10]

More importantly in Ukraine's case the Final Act was supplemented by the four-power agreement of December 1994, which reiterated its provisions on frontiers. After the collapse of the Soviet Union, Ukraine and other parts of the former Soviet Union were left with dozens of nuclear weapons undermining international efforts to prevent their spread to more states. To encourage Kiev and the other successor states to transfer these to Russia, the governments in Washington, Moscow and London guaranteed that they would not infringe their integrity and independence. The three powers also agreed that they would respond if Ukraine and the others were threatened with nuclear weapons yet Putin claimed in March 2015 that he was ready to put Russian nuclear forces on alert during the Crimean crisis, an action that would have drastically escalated the tensions and even more drastically infringed the agreement.[11]

Intervention in Ukraine not only undermined the Final Act and made a mockery of the four-power agreement but it also damaged the Nuclear Non-Proliferation Treaty. Even though it would have been very difficult, if not impossible, for Ukraine to operate and maintain the missiles, in the future a state being encouraged by the international community to abandon its ambitions to acquire nuclear weapons will not be reassured by any guarantees for its independence except the presence of substantial friendly forces on its territory.[12] It was hardly surprising that North Korea clung to its nuclear programme in 2017 and refused to give it up despite US nuclear threats.

Unfortunately, each time Putin has broken international agreements and challenged the West he has cemented his popularity in his own country as these assertions of his power apparently compensate for the humiliations of the past and divert attention from Russia's economic problems. In August 2015 Pew reported that 88 % of Russians supported their President. The cost was reputational; only in China and Vietnam were majorities elsewhere favourable to Moscow, while in Africa, Europe, Latin America and Asia-Pacific strong majorities preferred the United States to Russia, and distrusted Putin himself.[13] Whenever criticisms were made of Russian behaviour Putin claimed that they were just another case of the West's historic policy of victimising his country. This was, for example, the Russian reaction in November 2015, when the World Anti-Doping Agency published a report showing that the Russian authorities were deeply involved in the widespread use of drugs by their athletes to enhance their performance.[14] Five months later when the leak of documents from a Panamanian company implicated Putin's associates in money laundering he claimed that it was another American plot to destabilise Russia even though many politicians elsewhere were just as embarrassed by the revelations.[15]

Meanwhile, on the other side of the world, China was in dispute with the states bordering the South China Sea over ownership of various atolls and islands in the area. This is, in part, an argument over history. The Chinese say that they were the first to 'discover' and lay claim to the Sea; other littoral states argue that the situation is governed by international laws developed over the years. However, as pointed out earlier, Chinese leaders have been encouraging their people to recall their 'century of humiliation' from the 1840s to the 1940s and particularly to berate the Japanese for their predecessors' attacks in the 1930s. With its people angered by past humiliation Beijing refused to join in the extensive arbitration procedures under the Law of the Sea apparently because it saw such institutions as Western creations, because it rightly feared it might lose and because it preferred to deal with individual nations directly rather than in a multinational forum where its power could not be brought to bear. Over recent years China has negotiated a series of territorial settlements with all but one of its many landward neighbours including Russia although significantly its border with one of the most powerful ones, India, remains disputed.[16] These agreements represented major diplomatic achievements for Beijing but they were also a reflection of its growing strength. Most of China's landward neighbours are economically and militarily feeble, and have no protector to ask for support. Commentators have pointed out that there was a tendency for the proportion of the disputed land handed to China in the various compromises to be greater the weaker the other state.[17] In 2013 Philippines asked an arbitration tribunal under the Law of the Sea Conference to rule on their maritime dispute with China and in July 2016 the Court affirmed that China's claims were unfounded.[18]

While the leaders of the Great Powers all maintain in 2017 that their countries are victimised rather than victimisers, the European nations are torn apart by their sympathies for other nations and particularly for those suffering from the wars in Syria, Iraq and Libya. More graphically and immediately than they have ever done in the past, televisions bring publics nightly pictures of the obliteration of towns and villages, the flight of terrified civilians and the fate of refugees rotting for months or even years in tented camps with no idea what the future will bring. Some, indeed, become slaves and are traded in markets in Libya in an horrific relapse into past barbarism. One-fifth, or even one-quarter of the people from nine countries now live abroad usually after being driven out by war, unrest or poverty.[19] Since the Second World War empathy has led to the proliferation of non-governmental organisations and charities to help the victims of war, earthquake, famine or plague in distant lands. It has encouraged the expansion of UN peacekeeping forces which try to save lives by helping to 'freeze' conflicts across Africa and in Cyprus and elsewhere. But the wars in the Middle East divide European opinion between those whose sympathies lie with the victims and want them to be allowed to come to Europe and those who fear that they will bring their quarrels and angers with them, commit acts of terrorism and overburden the social services. In its December 2016 paper Pew reported that 59 % of Europeans believed that admitting such refugees would increase the risk of terrorism in their country.[20] Of Spaniards, 93 % and 91 % of French expressed concerns about the threat from the Islamic State with the median level of fear across the region being 76 %.

Thus, while revisionists complain that their own country is or was a victim to unite their people and depersonalise potential enemies, empathy divides other nations. Maverick political parties have gained credibility because they can excite national empathy by representing their countrymen as the victims and depersonalising foreigners. To Russian and Chinese leaders Western liberal governments may appear weak just as they did in the 1930s. In contrast to the euphoric idea that democracy was now the only living political ideology which was prevalent in the West at the end of the Cold War, conventional, democratic politicians are disparaged in Europe and the United States.[21] According to Pew's October 2017 poll only 40 % of Americans and Australians and 36 % of Britons and French were committed democrats unwilling to consider any other form of government.[22]

This is where historians might become politically of some significance. They can point out that the 'great seesaw' between optimism and pessimism is always swinging in open, democratic societies and that Western confidence will recover after the 2008 financial crisis. Internationally they can admit the truth of many of the complaints from the revisionists while pointing out that they are not the whole picture. Russia has suffered terribly from invasions from the West, China was subject to a century of humiliation and brutal interventions, the United States has carried the burden of acting as the stabilising world power since 1945 while many of its citizens suffer from poor social services. But some western nations led by Britain and later the United States did their best to help Russia in each great war against its enemies, similarly Japan attacked the United States and Britain in December 1941 in large part because they would not accept Tokyo's colonial expansion in China and Southeast Asia. The United States was defending its own interests as well as European and others when it set up the post-1945 international system. Above all, historians can remind politicians of the complexity of analogies before they make decisions, the dangers of using victimhood to demonise other nations and the length of time that nations now harbour resentments about the past.

## Notes

1. See the excellent analysis by Roland Stromberg, *Redemption by War: The Intellectuals and 1914*, Regents Press of Kansas, Lawrence, 1982.
2. Paul Kennedy, *Preparing for the Twenty-First Century*, Harper/Collins, London, 1993, pp. 290–308. See also Kennedy's earlier book, *The Rise and Fall of the Great Powers: Economic Change and Political Conflict from 1500 to 2000*, Unwin Hyman, London, 1988, pp. 514–535. See also 'NHS holds top spot in healthcare survey', *Guardian*, 14 July 2017.
3. 'Under Mr Trump, America Surrenders', *New York Times*, 16 October 2017.
4. See, for example, 'Trumponomics', *The Economist*, 13 May 2017, pp. 20–24. For a defence of the North Atlantic Free Trade Area by Gordon Ritchie, former Canadian Ambassador for Trade see 'Trump and Trade', *The Economist*, 3 June 2017, p. 18.

5. 'Dictators join Putin's victory parade', *Sunday Times*, 10 May 2015; 'China military parade shows might as Xi Jinpeng pledges 300,000 cut in army', *The Guardian* on line, 3 September 2015.
6. BBC World Service Poll, 4 July 2014. Note Israel has never admitted that it has nuclear weapons but this is widely believed to be the case.
7. See, for example, Arkady N. Shevchenko, *Breaking with Moscow*, Grafton, London, 1986, pp. 153, 452, 459.
8. IISS, *Military Balance 1998/1999*, Oxford University Press/IISS, London, 1998, pp. 53 and 108.
9. A classic history of the conference was written by John J. Maresca who served on the US delegation throughout its deliberations. See J. J. Maresca, *To Helsinki: The Conference on Security and Co-operation in Europe, 1973–1975*, Duke University Press, Durham, 1987, pp. 110–116.
10. *Conference on Security and Co-operation in Europe: Final Act*, HMSO, London, Cmnd 6198, August 1975, p. 3.
11. 'Russia was ready to put nuclear forces on alert over Crimea, Putin says', CNN, 16 March 2015, http://edition.cnn.com/2015/03/16/europe/russia/putin-crime.
12. Maria Rose Rublee, 'Fantasy Counterfactual: A Nuclear-Armed Ukraine', *Survival*, April–May 2015, p. 145.
13. 'Russia, Putin held in low regard around the world', Pew Research Center, 5 August 2015 and 16 August 2017. See also 'How to understand Putin's jaw droppingly high approval ratings', *Washington Post*, 6 March 2016.
14. 'Doping in sport: A Cold-war chill' and 'Tamper Proof: Russia's Olympian drug habit', *The Economist*, 14 November 2015 pp. 39 and 23 July 2016, p. 25.
15. Mike Eckel, 'Putin says Panama papers part of a plan to destabilise Russia', Radio Free Europe, 7 April 2016.
16. Bruce A Elleman, Stephen Kotkin and Clive Scofield, Editors, *Beijing's Power and Chinese Borders: Twenty Neighbours in Asia*, Sharpe, New York, 2013, pp. 47–60.
17. Elleman, Kotkin and Schofield, 'Conclusion' in Elleman et al., *Beijing's Power*, p. 311.
18. 'In victory for Philippines, Hague Court to hear dispute over South China Sea', *New York Times*, 30 October 2015 and 'Courting trouble', *The Economist*, 16 July 2016, p. 47.
19. 'In nine countries, 20 % or more born there have migrated or sought refuge abroad', Pew Research Center, 10 November 2016.
20. '4 factors driving anti-establishment sentiment in Europe', Pew Research Center, 6 December 2016.
21. For the euphoria after the Cold War see particularly Francis Fukuyama, *The End of History and the Last Man*, Hamish Hamilton, London, 1992. For

later comments on democracy see 'The debasing of American politics', *The Economist*, 15 December 2016. For a general theory of the seesaw between Western optimism and pessimism see Geoffrey Blainey, *The Great Seesaw: A New View of the Western World, 1750–2000*, Macmillan, Basingstoke, 1988.
22. 'Globally broad support for representative and direct democracy but many also endorse nondemocratic alternatives', Pew Research Center, 16 October 2017.

# BIBLIOGRAPHY

Adams Michael, Editor, *The Middle East: A Handbook*, Anthony Blond, London, 1971.
Adelman Jonathan R., *Revolution, Armies and War: A Political History*, Lynne Rienner, Boulder, Colorado, 1985.
Albright Madeleine, *Madam Secretary: A Memoir*, Macmillan, London, 2003.
Ambrose Stephen, *Eisenhower: The President*, George Allen and Unwin, London, 1984.
Andrew Christopher and Gordievski Oleg, *KGB: The Inside Story*, Hodder and Stoughton, London, 1990.
Annan Noel, *Changing Enemies: The Defeat and Regeneration of Germany*, Harper/Collins, London, 1995.
Anonymous, *A Woman in Berlin: Diary 20 April 1945 to 22 June 1945*, Virago, London, 2006.
Applebaum Anne, *Iron Curtain: The Crushing of Eastern Europe*, Penguin, London, 2013.
Armitage M. J., and Mason R. A., *Airpower in the Nuclear Age 1945–1984*, Macmillan, Basingstoke, 1985.
Ashford Sheena and Timms Noel, *What Europe Thinks: A Study of Western European Values*, Dartmouth, Aldershot, 1992.
Asprey Robert B., *War in the Shadows: The Guerrilla in History*, Doubleday, New York, 1975.
Association of History Masters in Secondary Schools, *The Teaching of History in Secondary Schools*, Cambridge University Press, London, 1965 edition.
Badsey Stephen, Editor, *The Media and International Security*, Frank Cass, London, 2000.

Barkan Elazar and Kar Alexander, Editors, *Taking Wrongs Seriously*, Stanford University Press, Stanford, 2006.
Barkan Elazar, *The Guilt of Nations: Restitution and Negotiating Historical Injustices*, Norton, New York, 2000.
Bakir V. and Barlow David M., Editors, *Communication in the Age of Suspicion: Trust and the Media*, Palgrave, Basingstoke, 2007.
Barraclough Geoffrey, *An Introduction to Contemporary History*, Penguin, Harmondsworth, 1973.
Barraclough Geoffrey, *History in a Changing World*, Oxford, 1955.
Barros James and Gregor Richard, *Double Deception: Stalin, Hitler and the Invasion of Russia*, Northern Illinois University Press, DeKalb, 1995.
Bass Gary J., *Freedom's Battle: The Origins of Humanitarian Intervention*, Knopf, New York, 2008.
Becker Carl, *Everyman his Own Historian: Essays on History and Politics*, Appleton-Century-Crofts, New York, 1935.
Beckett Andy, *Pinochet in Piccadilly: Britain and Chile's Secret History*, Faber and Faber, London, 2002.
Beloff Max, *The Balance of Power*, George Allen and Unwin, London, 1968.
Bennett Gordon A. and Montaperto Ronald N., *Red Guard: The Political Biography of Dai Hsiao-ai*, George Allen and Unwin, London, 1971.
Benze James G., *Nancy Reagan: On the White House Stage*, University Press of Kansas, Lawrence, 2002.
Berlin Isaiah, *The Crooked Timber of Humanity: Chapters in the History of Ideas*, Pimlico, London, 2013.
Bertram Thomas, *Alarms and Excursions in Arabia*, George Allen and Unwin, London, 1931.
Blainey Geoffrey, *The Causes of Wars*, Sun Books, Melbourne, 1977.
Blainey Geoffrey, *The Great Seesaw*, Macmillan, Basingstoke, 1988.
Blake George, *No Other Choice: An Autobiography*, Jonathan Cape, London, 1990.
Bland Douglas D., *Time Bomb: Canada and the First Nations*, Dundurn, Toronto, 2014.
Blumenfeld Laura, *Revenge: A Story of Hope*, Picador, London, 2002.
Boemeke M. F., Feldman F and Glaser Elizabeth, *The Treaty of Versailles: A Reassessment after 75 Years*, German Historical Institute/Cambridge University Press, Cambridge, 1998.
Bond Brian, *The Unquiet Western Front: Britain's Role in Literature and History*, Cambridge University Press, Cambridge, 2002.
Bouchard Gerard, Editor, *National Myths: Constructed Pasts, Contested Presents*, Routledge, New York, 2013.
Bower Tom, *Blind Eye to Murder: Britain, America and the Purging of Nazi Germany- a Pledge Betrayed*, Granada, London, 1983.

Bower Tom, *The Paperclip Conspiracy: The Battle for the Secrets of Nazi Germany*, Paladin, London, 1988a.
Boyd Carl, *Hitler's Japanese Confidant: General Oshima Hiroshi and Magic Intelligence, 1941–1945*, University Press of Kansas, Lawrence, 1993.
Brocklehurst Helen, *Who's Afraid of Children: Children, Conflict and International Relations*, Ashgate, Aldershot, 2006.
Burns-Bisogno Louisa, *Censoring Irish Nationalism: The British, Irish and American Suppression of Republican Images in Film and Television 1905–1995*, McFarland, Jefferson, North Carolina, 1997.
Buruma Ian, *Wages of Guilt: Memories of War in Germany and Japan*, Vintage, London, 1995.
Butterfield H, *Christianity and History*, G. Bell, London, 1949.
Byford-Jones W., *Berlin Twilight*, Hutchinson, London, undated.
Cantril Hadley and Strunk Mildred, *Public Opinion 1935–1946*, Princeton University Press, Princeton, 1951.
Caplan Neil, *The Israeli-Palestine Conflict: Contested Histories*, Wiley-Blackwell, Chichester, 2010.
Carr E. H., *Conditions of Peace*, Macmillan, London, 1942.
Carr E. H., *What is History?* Penguin, Harmondsworth, 1964.
Castile George Pierre, *Taking Charge: Native American Self-Determination and Federal Indian Policy, 1975–1993*, University of Arizona Press, Tucson, 2006.
Catton Bruce, *Prefaces to History*, Doubleday, New York, 1970.
Caute David, *The Fellow Travellers: Intellectual Friends of Communism*, Yale University Press, New Haven, 1988.
Chamberlain William Henry, *Japan over Asia*, Duckworth, London, 1938.
Chaudhuri Nirad C., *Thy Hand Great Anarch! India 1921–1952*, Chatto and Windus, London, 1987 and Hogarth Press, London, 1990.
Churchill Winston, *The Second World War: Volume 11, Their Finest Hour*, Reprint Society, London, 1951.
Cienciala Anna M., Lebedeva Natalia S. and Materski Wojciech, *Katyn: A Crime Without Punishment*, Yale University Press, New Haven, 2007.
Clough Ralph, *Embattled Korea: The Rivalry for International Support*, Westview Press, Boulder, 1987.
Coker, Christopher, *Waging War without Warriors*, Lynne Rienner Publishers, Boulder 2002.
Cole Alyson M., *The Cult of True Victimhood: From the War on Welfare to the War on Terror*, Stanford University Press, Stanford, 2007.
Coleman David and Salt John, *Patterns, Trends and Processes*, Oxford University Press, Oxford, 1992.
Collingwood R.G., *The Idea of History*, Oxford Paperbacks, Oxford University Press, London, 1961.
Collins Eamon and McGovern Mick, *Killing Rage*, Granta, London, 1997.

Conquest Robert, *The Great Terror: Stalin's Purge of the Thirties*, Pelican. Harmondsworth, 1971.
Craig Gordon A. and George Alexander L., *Force and Statecraft: Diplomatic Problems of Our Time*, Oxford University Press, New York, 1995.
Curzon Marquess of Kedleston, *Tales of Travel*, Hodder and Stoughton, London, 1923.
David Richard, Editor, *Hakluyt's Voyages*, Chatto and Windus, London, 1981.
De Cuellar Javier Perez, *Pilgrimage for Peace*, Macmillan, Basingstoke, 1997.
Delaney Enda, *The Curse of Reason: The Great Irish Famine*, Gill and Macmillan, Dublin, 2012.
Dicey A. V., *Law and Public Opinion in England during the 19$^{th}$ Century*, Macmillan, London, 1962.
Dikotter Frank, *Mao's Great Famine: The History of China's Most Devastating Catastrophe 1958–1962*, Bloomsbury, London, 2011.
Djilas Milovan, *Land without Justice: An Autobiography of his Youth*, Methuen, London, 1958.
Donald Sir Robert, *The Tragedy of Trianon: Hungary's Appeal to Humanity*, Thornton Butterworth, London, 1928.
Dorman Andrew M. *Blair's Successful War: British Military Intervention in Sierra Leone*, Ashgate, Farnham, 2009.
Draper Alfred, *The Amritsar Massacre: Twilight of the Raj*, Buchan and Enright, London, 1985
Eden Sir Anthony, *Full Circle*, Cassell, London, 1960.
Einzig Paul, *The Japanese "New Order" in Asia*, Macmillan, London, 1943.
Elleman Bruce A, Kotkin Stephen and Scofield Clive, Editors, *Beijing's Power and Chinese Borders: Twenty Neighbours in Asia*, Sharpe, New York, 2013.
Elon Amos and Hassan Sana, *Between Enemies: An Arab-Israeli Dialogue*, Andre Deutsch, London, 1974.
Eltis David and Richardson David, Editors, *Routes to Slavery: Direction, Ethnicity and Mortality in the Atlantic Slave Trade*, Frank Cass, London, 1997.
Elton G. R., *Return to Essentials: Some Reflections on the Present State of Historical Study*, Cambridge University Press, Cambridge 1991.
Equiano Olaudah, *The Interesting Narrative of the Life of Olaudah Equiano written by Himself*, St Martin's Press, Boston, 1995.
Fairweather Jack, *The Good War: Why We Couldn't Win the War or the Peace in Afghanistan*, Jonathan Cape, London, 2014.
Fisher Roger and Ury William, *Getting to Yes: Negotiating an Agreement without Giving In*, Business Books, London, 1991.
Freedman Lawrence, Editor, *Military Intervention in European Conflicts*, Blackwell Publishers, Oxford, 1994.
Fujitani T., White Geoffrey and Yoneyama Lisa, *Perilous Memories: The Asian Pacific War(s)*, Duke University Press, Duke, 2001.

Fuller J. F. C., *The Dragon's Den: A Study of War and Peace*, Constable, London, 1932.
Furedi Frank, *Authority: A Sociological History*, Cambridge University Press, Cambridge, 2013a.
Furniss Elizabeth, *The Burden of History: Colonialism and the Frontier Myth in a Rural Canadian Community*, UBC Press, Vancouver, 1999.
Fussell Paul, *Killing in Verse and Prose and Other Essays*, Bellew, London, 1990.
Gemie Sharif, Reid Fiona and Humbert Laure, *Outcast Europe: Relief and Relief Workers in an Era of Total War 1936–48*, Continuum, London, 2012.
Gibney Mark, Howard-Hassmann Rhoda et al, Editors, *The Age of Apology: Facing up to the Past*, University of Pennsylvania, Philadelphia, 2008.
Gillespie Richard, *Soldiers of Peron: Argentina's Montoneros*, Clarendon, Oxford, 1982.
Gillies Midge, *Waiting for Hitler: Voices from Britain on the Brink of Invasion*, Hodder and Stoughton, London, 2006.
Gimpel Jean, *The Medieval Machine: The Industrial Revolution of the Middle Ages*, Gollancz, London, 1976.
Gobodo-Madikizela Pumla and Van Der Merve Chris, *Memory, Narrative and Forgiveness: Perspectives on the Unfinished Journeys of the Past*, Cambridge Scholars, Newcastle, 2009.
Goldstone Jack A, Kaufman Eric P. and Tofte Monica Duffy, *Political Demography*, Oxford University Press, Oxford, 2012
Gollancz Victor, Editor, *What would be the Character of a New War*, Gollancz, London, 1933.
Golway Terry, Editor, *Words that Ring through Time*, Overlook, New York, 2009.
Grey Peter, *The Irish Famine*, Thames and Hudson, London. 1995.
Griffin David Ray, *The 9/11 Commission Report: Omissions and Distortions*, Arris, Moreton-in-Marsh, 2005.
Haig Alexander M, *Caveat: Realism, Reagan and Foreign Policy*, Weidenfeld and Nicolson, London, 1984.
Halberstam David, *War in a Time of Peace: Bush, Clinton and the Generals*, Bloomsbury, London, 2002.
Haldane Aylmer, *The Autobiography of General Sir Aylmer Haldane*, William Blackwood, Edinburgh, 1948.
Harari Yuval Noah, *Renaissance Military Memoirs: War, History and Identity, 1450–1600*, Boydell Press, Woodbridge, 2004.
Harrison Mark, *The Economics of World War II*, Cambridge University Press, Cambridge, 1998.
Harrisson Tom and Madge Charles, *War Begins at Home*, Chatto and Windus, London, 1940.
Hastings Max, *Going to the Wars*, Macmillan, Basingstoke, 2000.
Hastings Max, *All Hell Let Loose: The World at War 1939–1945*, HarperCollins, London, 2012.

Hayek, F. A., *Capitalism and the Historians*, Routledge, London, 2003.
Hein Laura and Selden Mark, Editors, *Censoring History: Citizenship and Memory in Japan, Germany and the United States*, M. E. Sharpe, Armonk, New York, 2000.
Herbert Ulrich, *Hitler's Foreign Workers: Enforced Foreign Labour in Germany under the Third Reich*, Cambridge University Press, Cambridge, 1997.
Herr Michael, *Dispatches*, Alfred A. Knopf, New York, 1977.
Hickman John, *News from the End of the World*, Hurst, London, 1998.
Hinsley F. H., *Power and the Pursuit of Peace: Theory and Practice in the History of International Relations between States*, Cambridge University Press, Cambridge, 1963.
Hoensch Jorg, *A History of Modern Hungary*, Longman, London, 1988.
Hofstadter Richard, *Anti-Intellectualism in American Life*, Vintage Books, New York, 1963.
Home Lord, *The Way the Wind Blows: An Autobiography*, Collins, London, 1976.
Hooker Virginia and Saikal Amin, Editors, *Islamic Perspectives on the New Millennium*, Institute of Southeast Asian Studies, Singapore, 2004.
Horstmann Lali, *Nothing for Tears*, Weidenfeld and Nicolson, London, 1999.
Howard Michael and Paret Peter, Editors, Carl von Clausewitz, *On War*, Princeton, New Jersey, 1984.
Hurd Douglas, *Memoirs*, Little Brown, London, 2003.
Hurst Michael, *Key Treaties of the Great Powers: 1814–1914*, David and Charles, Newton Abbot, 1972.
Hutchinson John, *The Dynamics of Cultural Nationalism: The Gaelic Revival and the Creation of the Irish National State*, Allen and Unwin, London, 1987.
Hyoe Murakami, *Japan: The Years of Trial and Hope: 1919–52*, Kodansha International, Tokyo, 1983.
Inge William Ralph, *England*, Hodder and Stoughton, London, 1938.
Ingham Bernard, *Kill the Messenger*, Harper/Collins, London, 1991.
Ishimaru Tota, *Japan Must Fight Britain*, Paternoster Library, London, 1936.
Israelyan Victor, *Inside the Kremlin during the Yom Kippur War*, Pennsylvania University Press, Pennsylvania, 1995.
Jalland Pat, *Death in War and Peace: Loss and Grief in England: 1914–1970*, Oxford University Press, Oxford, 2010.
Jameson Storm, *Journey from the North: The Autobiography of Storm Jameson*, Virago, London, 1984.
Jenkins T. A., *Sir Robert Peel*, Macmillan, Basingstoke, 1999.
Jenner W. J. F., *The Tyranny of History*, Allen Lane, London, 1992.
Jordan Ulrike, Editor, *Conditions of Surrender: Britons and Germans Witness the End of the Second* World War, Tauris, London, 1997
Kagan, Robert, *Of Paradise and Power: America and Europe in the New World Order*, Knopf, New York, 2003.

Kahneman Daniel, *Thinking Fast and Slow*, Allen Lane/Penguin, London, 2011.
Kaplan Robert D., *Balkan Ghosts: A Journey Through History*, St Martin's Press, New York, 1993.
Karsh Efraim, *Fabricating Israeli History: The 'New Historians'*, Frank Cass, London, 1997.
Keeley Lawrence H., *War Before Civilization: The Myth of the Peaceful Savage*, Oxford University Press, New York, 1996.
Kelidar Abbas, *The Integration of Modern Iraq*, Croom Helm, London, 1979.
Kelley Kitty, *Nancy Reagan: The Unauthorised Biography*, Bantam Press, London, 1991.
Kennedy Paul, *The Rise and Fall of the Great Powers: Economic Change and Military Conflict from 1500 to 2000*, Unwin Hyman, London, 1988.
Kennedy Paul, *Preparing for the Twenty-First Century*, Harper/Collins, London, 1993.
Keynes John Maynard, *The Economic Consequences of the Peace*, Harcourt, Brace and Howe, New York, 1920.
Khrushchev N., *Khrushchev Remembers*, Andre Deutsch, London, 1971.
Kilcullen David, *The Accidental Guerrilla: Fighting Small Wars in the Midst of a Big One*, Hurst, London, 2009.
Kim Mikyoung and Schwartz Barry, Editors, *Northeast Asia's Difficult Past: Essays in Collective Memory*, Palgrave/Macmillan, Basingstoke, 2010.
Klein Herbert S., *The Atlantic Slave Trade*, Cambridge University Press, Cambridge, 2010.
Knight Roger, *The Pursuit of Victory: The Life and Achievement of Horatio Nelson*, Allen Lane, London, 2005.
Korboniski Stefan, *Warsaw in Exile*, George Allen and Unwin, London, 1966.
Laqueur, Walter, *Guerrilla: A Historical and Critical Study*, Weidenfeld and Nicolson, London, 1977.
Ledwidge Frank, *Investment in Blood: The Real Cost of Britain's Afghan War*, Yale University Press, New Haven, 2013b.
Lemish Defra and Gotz Maya, Editors, *Children and the Media in War and Conflict*, Hampton Press, Creskill, New Jersey, 2007.
Lerner Robert, Nagai Althea K and Rothman Stanley, *Molding the Good Citizen: The Politics of High School History Texts*, Praeger, Westport, Connecticut, 1999.
Levstik Linda S and Barton Keith C., *Researching History Education: Theory, Method and Context*, Routledge, New York, 2008.
Lincoln Bruce, *Authority: Construction and Coercion*, University of Chicago Press, Chicago, 1996.
Linenthal Edward and Engelhardt Tom, *History Wars: The Enola Gay and Other Battles for the American Past*, Metropolitan Books/Henry Holt, New York, 1996.

Ling Ken, *Red Guard: Schoolboy to 'Little General' in Mao's China*, Macdonald, London, 1972.
Lloyd Selwyn, *Suez 1956: A Personal Account*, Coronet, Sevenoaks, 1980.
Lloyd George David, *War Memoirs*, Odhams, London, 1938.
Ludi Regula, *Reparations for Nazi Victims in Postwar Europe*, Cambridge University Press, Cambridge, 2012.
Luong Hy V., *Tradition, Revolution, and Market Economy in a North Vietnamese Village, 1925–2006*, University of Hawai'i Press, Honolulu, 2010.
Lyons F. S. L., *Culture and Anarchy in Ireland*, Clarendon Press, Oxford, 1979.
Macintyre Stuart and Clark Anna, *The History Wars*, Melbourne University Press, Melbourne, 2004.
Madge Charles and Harrisson Tom, *First Year's Work 1937–38*, Lindsay Drummond, London, 1938.
Major John, *The Autobiography*, HarperCollins, London, 1999.
Mahnken Thomas, Maiolo Joseph and Stevenson David, Editors, *Arms Races in International Politics from the Nineteenth to the Twenty-First Century*, Oxford University Press, Oxford, 2016,
Mantoux Etienne, *The Carthaginian Peace or The Economic Consequences of Mr Keynes*, Geoffrey Cumberlege/Oxford University Press, London, 1946.
Maresca John J. *To Helsinki: The Conference on Security and Cooperation in Europe, 1973–1975*, Duke University Press, Durham, 1987.
Margach James, *Abuse of Power: The War between Downing Street and the Media from Lloyd George to Callaghan*, W. H. Allen, London, 1978.
Mason Philip, *A Matter of Honour: An Account of the Indian Army Its Officers and Men*, Penguin, Harmondsworth, 1976.
McCallum R. B., *Public Opinion and the Last Peace*, Oxford University Press, London, 1944.
McClelland Grigor, *Embers of War: Letters from a Quaker Relief Worker in War-Torn Germany*, Tauris, London, 1997.
McLaren Moray, *The Scots*, Penguin, Harmondsworth, 1951.
Mearsheimer John, *Why Leaders Lie: The Truth about Lying in International Politics*, Duckwoth Overlook, London, 2011.
Meehan Patricia, *A Strange Enemy People: Germans under British Rule, 1945–1950*, Peter Owen, London, 2001.
Melton V, *From Versailles to Mers el-Kebir*, Naval Institute Press, Annapolis, 2015.
Miller Hugh, *First Impressions of England and Its People*, William P. Nimmo, Edinburgh, 1869.
Miller, Manhari Chatterjee, *Wronged by Empire: Post-Imperial Ideology and Foreign Policy in India and China*, Stanford University Press, Stanford, 2013.
Mitter Rana, *China's War with Japan: The Struggle for Survival 1937–1945*, Penguin, London, 2014.
Moffat Alistair, *The British A Genetic Journey*, Virlinn, Edinburgh, 2013.

Morgan J. H., *Assize of Arms: Being the Story of Germany and her Rearmament 1919–1939*, Methuen, London, 1945.
Morgenthau Hans J., *Truth and Power: Essays of a Decade 1960–1970*, Pall Mall, London, 1970
Morgenthau Henry with Strother French, *I Was Sent to Athens*, Doubleday, Doran, New York, 1929.
Morgenthau Henry, *Secrets of the Bosphorus*, Hutchinson, London, 1919.
Morgenthau Henry, *Ambassador Morgenthau's Story*, Gomidas Institute, Ann Arbor, 2000.
Morris-Suzuki Tessa, Low Morris, Petrov Peonid and Tsu Timothy Y, *East Asia beyond the History Wars: Confronting the Ghosts of Violence*, Routledge, London, 2013.
Murphy David E., *What Stalin Knew: The Enigma of Barbarossa*, Yale University Press, New Haven, 2005.
Namier Sir Lewis, *Vanished Supremacies*, Penguin, Harmondsworth, 1962.
Nee Victor and Layman Dan, *The Cultural Revolution at Peking University*, Monthly Review, New York, 1969.
Nicolson Harold, *Peacemaking 1919*, Constable, London, 1933.
Nixon Richard, *The Memoirs of Richard Nixon*, Sidgwick and Jackson, London 1978.
Nixon Richard, *1999: Victory without War*, Sidgwick and Jackson, London, 1988.
O'Brien Conor Cruise, *States of Ireland*, Hutchinson, London, 1972.
Olmsted Kathryn S, *Real Enemies: Conspiracy Theories and American Democracy: World War 1 to 9/11*, Oxford University Press, New York, 2009.
Olinisakin Funmi, *Peacekeeping in Sierra Leone: The Story of UNAMISIL*, Lynne Rienner, Boulder, 2008.
Palmer Alan, *The Lands Between: A History of East-Central Europe since the Congress of Vienna*, Weidenfeld and Nicolson, London, 1970.
Pares Bernard, *The Historian's Business and Other Essays*, Clarendon, Oxford, 1961.
Parillo Mark, *The Japanese Merchant Marine in World War 11*, Naval Institute Press, Annapolis, 1993.
Parke H. W. and Wormell D. E. W., *The Delphic Oracle*, Basil Blackwell, Oxford, 1956.
Pedwell Carolyn, *Affective Relations: The Transnational Politics of Empathy*, Palgrave Macmillan, 2014.
Pennell Catriona, *A Kingdom United: Popular Responses to the Outbreak of the First World War in Britain and Ireland*, Oxford University Press, Oxford, 2012.
Petrie Sir Charles, *Twenty Years' Armistice-And After: British Foreign Policy since 1918*, Eyre and Spottiswoode, London, 1940.
Philby Kim, *My Silent War*, Granada, London, 1969.

Phillips Joshua E. E. *None of Us were Like This Before: American Soldiers and Torture*, Verso, London, 2010.
PipesDaniel, *Conspiracy*, Free Press, New York, 1999.
Playne C. E., *The Pre-War Mind in Britain*, George Allen and Unwin, London, 1925.
Podeh Elie, *The Arab-Israeli Conflict in Israeli History Textbooks: 1948–2000*, Bergin and Garvey, Westport, 2002.
Popper Karl R., *The Poverty of Historicism*, Routledge/Kegan/Paul, London, 1957.
Powell Colin with Joseph Persico, *My American Journey*, Ballantine, New York, 1996.
Pronay Nicholas and Wilson Keith, *The Political Re-Education of Germany and her Allies after World War 11*, Croom Helm, London, 1985.
Race Jeffrey, *War Comes to Long An: Revolutionary Conflict in a Vietnamese Village*, University of California Press, Berkeley, 1972.
Raghavan Srinath, *India's War: The Making of Modern South Asia 1939–1945*, Allen Lane, 2016.
Ranelagh John, *The Agency: The Rise and Decline of the CIA*, Hodder and Stoughton, London, 1986.
Raviv Amiram, Oppenheimer Louis, Bar-Tal Daniel, Editors, *How Children Understand War and Peace*, Jossey-Bass, Publishers, San Francisco, 1999.
Reed Thomas C, *At the Abyss: An Insider's History of the Cold War*, Random House, New York, 2004.
Riddell Lord, *Lord Riddell's Intimate Diary of the Peace Conference and After: 1918–1923*, Victor Gollancz, London, 1933.
Rifkin Jeremy, *The Empathetic Civilization: The Race to Global Consciousness in a World in Crisis*, Polity, Cambridge, 1988.
Roger Fisher and William Ury, *Getting to Yes: Negotiating an Agreement without Giving In*, Business Books, London, 1991.
Rogers Simon Editor, *The Hutton Inquiry and Its Impact*, Politico's Guardian Books, London, 2004.
Sacks, Jonathan, *The Great Partnership: God, Science and the Search for Meaning*, Hodder, London, 2011.
Sandars C. T., *America's Overseas Garrisons: The Leasehold Empire*, Oxford University Press, 2000.
Schlosser Eric, *Command and Control*, Penguin, London, 2014.
Schoen Douglas E., *The End of Authority: How a Loss of Legitimacy and Broken Trust are Endangering our Future*, Rowman and Littlefield, Lanham, Maryland, 2013.
Shawcross William, *The Shah's Last Ride: The Story of the Exile, Misadventures and Death of the Emperor*, Chatto and Windus, London, 1989.
Shayakhmetov Mukhamet, *The Silent Steppe: The Memoir of a Kazakh Nomad under Stalin*, Rookery, New York, 2006.

Sheehan James, *The Monopoly of Violence: Why Europeans Hate Going to War*, Faber and Faber, London, 2008.
Sheridan Dorothy, *Wartime Women: A Mass-Observation Anthology 1937–1945*, Phoenix Press, London, 2000.
Shevchenko Arkady, *Breaking with Moscow*, Grafton, London, 1986.
Shipman M. D., *Education and Modernisation*, Faber and Faber, London, 1971.
Shudo, *The Nanking Massacre: Fact Versus Fiction*, Sekai Shuppan, Tokyo, 2005.
Shultz George P., *Turmoil and Triumph: Diplomacy, Power and the Victory of the American Ideal*, Scribner, New York, 1993.
Shute Nevil, *What Happened to the Corbetts*, Heinemann, London, 1939.
Siegel Mona L., *The Moral Disarmament of France: Education, Pacifism, and Patriotism, 1914–1940*, Cambridge University Press, Cambridge, 2004.
Simms Brendan, *Unfinest Hour: Britain and the Destruction of Bosnia*, Allen Lane, The Penguin Press, London, 2001.
Simpson Emile, *War from the Ground Up; Twenty-First Century Combat as Politics*, Hurst, London, 2012.
Simpson John and Bennett Jana, *Voices from a Secret War*, Robson, London, 1985.
Skya Walter A, *Japan's Holy War: The Ideology of Radical Shinto Ultranationalism*, Duke University Press, Durham, 2009.
Snepp Frank, *Decent Interval: The American Debacle in Vietnam and the Fall of Saigon*, Penguin, Harmondsworth, 1980.
Solzhenitsyn Alexander, *The Gulag Archipelago: 1918–1956*, Collins/Fontana, London, 1974.
Southey Robert, *The Life of Nelson*, Hutchinson, London, 1905.
Spaight J. M., *Pseudo-Security*, Longmans, Green, London, 1928.
Spear Percival, *India, Pakistan and the West*, Oxford University Press, London, 1952.
Stafford R. S., *The Tragedy of the Assyrians*, George Allen and Unwin, London, 1935.
Stephenson Hugh, Editor, *Media Voices: The James Cameron Lectures*, Politicos, London, 2001.
Strang Lord, *Britain in World Affairs*, Faber and Faber and Andre Deutsch, London, 1961.
Straw Jack, *Last Man Standing: Memoirs of a Political Survivor*, Macmillan, London, 2012.
Stromberg Roland, *Redemption by War: The Intellectuals and 1914*, Regents Press of Kansas, Lawrence, 1982.
Sullivan Matthew Barry, *Threshold of Peace: Four Hundred Thousand German Prisoners and the People of Britain, 1944–1948*, Hamish Hamilton, London, 1979.
Sykes J. B., Editor, *The Concise Oxford English Dictionary*, Clarendon, Oxford, 1986.

Taylor Philip M., *Munitions of the Mind: A History of Propaganda from the Ancient World to the Present Day*, Manchester University Press, Manchester 2003.
Thomson David, *Woodbrook*, Penguin, Harmondsworth, 1976.
Towle Philip and Kosuge Nobuko Margaret, *Britain and Japan in the Twentieth Century*, I.B.Tauris, London, 2007.
Tsuji Colonel Masanobu, *Singapore: The Japanese Version*, Constable, London, 1960.
Tutu Desmond, *No Future Without Forgiveness*, Rider, London, 1999.
Ulrich Herbart, *Hitler's Foreign Workers: Enforced Labour in Germany under the Third Reich*, Cambridge University Press, Cambridge, 1997.
Valery, Paul, *Reflections on the World Today*, Thames and Hudson, London, 1951.
Vance, J. D, *Hillbilly Elegy*, HarperCollins, New York, 2016.
Van Prooijen Jan-Willem and van Lange, Paul A. M., *Power, Politics and Paranoia*, Cambridge University Press, Cambridge, 2014.
Vassiltchikov Marie, *The Berlin Diaries 1940–1945*, Chatto and Windus, London, 1985.
Veve, T. D., *The Duke of Wellington and the British Army of Occupation in France, 1815–1818*, Greenwood Press, Westport, 1992.
Vickers Edward and Jones Alisa, *History Education and Identity in East Asia*, Routledge, New York, 2005.
Von Kardoff Ursula, *Diary of a Nightmare: Berlin 1942–1945*, Rupert Hart-Davis, London, 1965.
Wallis Joanne and Carr Andrew, Editors, *Asia-Pacific Security: An Introduction*, Georgetown University Press, Washington, 2016.
Walton Timothy, *Challenges in Intelligence Analysis: Lessons from 1300 BC to the Present*, Cambridge University Press, Cambridge, 2010.
Welch David A. *Justice and the Genesis of War*, Cambridge University Press, Cambridge, 1993.
West Rebecca, *Black Lamb and Grey Falcon: A Journey through Yugoslavia*, Macmillan, London, 1955 (first published 1942).
Williams A. T., *A Very British Killing: The Death of Baha Mousa*, Jonathan Cape, London, 2012.
Wilson, Arnold, *Mesopotamia 1917–1920: A Clash of Loyalties*, Oxford University Press, Oxford, 1931.
Wolfsfeld Gadi, *Media and the Path to Peace*, Cambridge University Press, Cambridge, 2004.
Woodward Bob, *Plan of Attack*, Simon and Schuster, London, 2004.
Woods Chris, *Sudden Justice: America's Secret Drone Wars*, Hurst, London, 2015.
Yoshihara Susan and Sylva Douglas A, Editors, *Population Decline and the Remaking of Great Power Politics*, Potomac Books, Washington, 2012.
Young Peter and Jesser Peter, *The Media and the Military*, Macmillan, Basingstoke, 1977.

Zamoyski, Adam, *Rites of Peace: The Fall of Napoleon and the Congress of Vienna*, Harper/Collins, London, 2007.
Ziegler Philip, *Mountbatten: The Official Biography*, Fontana/Collins, London, 1986.
Zimm Alan D., *Attack on Pearl Harbor: Strategy, Myths, Deceptions*, Casemate, Philadelphia, 2011.

## OFFICIAL PUBLICATIONS

*Palestine: Statement by His Majesty's Government, Official Communique* No 2/39, p. 3, quoting the Command Paper of 1922, Cmd 1700.
*Conference on Security and Co-operation in Europe: Final Act*, Cmnd 6198, HMSO, London, 1975.
*Report of the Warren Commission on the Assassination of President Kennedy*, Bantam, New York, 1964.
*The 9/11 Commission Report: Final Report of the National Commission on Terrorist Attacks upon the United States*, Norton, New York, 2004.

## SELECTED PUBLIC OPINION POLLS

'America's image further erodes; Europe wants weaker ties', Pew Research Center, 18 March 2003.
'Views of a Changing World 2003', Pew Research Center, 3 June 2003.
'Islamic extremism causes concern for Muslims and Western countries', Pew Global Attitudes Project, 14 July 2005.
'American' support for Israel unchanged by recent hostilities', Pew Research Center, 26 July 2006.
'Diminished public appetite for military force—Mideast oil', Pew Research Center, 6 September 2006.
Spring 2007 Survey, Pew Global Attitudes Project.
'Public wary of military intervention in Libya: Broad concern that the US is over-committed', Pew Research Center, 14 March 2011.
'China seen overtaking US as global superpower', Pew Research Center, 13 July 2011.
'From hyperpower to declining power', Pew Global Attitudes Project, 7 September 2011.
'The American-Western European values gap', Pew Research Center, 17 November 2011.
'Modest backing for Israel in Gaza crisis', Pew Research Center, 13 January 2013.
YouGov Poll 9–10 January 2013.
YouGov Survey, 27–29 January and 3–4 February 2013.

'Politicians trusted less than estate agents', Ipsos Mori, 15 February 2013.
YouGov Poll, 28–29 August 2013.
'9th Japan-China Public Opinion Poll', 13 August 2013, Genron NPO and China Daily.
'Americans believe US participation in Gulf War a decade ago worthwhile', Gallup News Service, 14 April 2014.
NBC News National Survey by Public Opinion Strategies/Hart Research Associates, 27–29 May 2014, Project 14353.
BBC World Service Poll by GlobeScan, 'Presentation of Results on Ratings of Different Countries', 4 July 2014, compiled by Gallup Pakistan.
'Public opinion in Pakistan in the year 1980', Gilani Research Foundation, 2 September 2014.
Gallup Pakistan Weekly Cyberletter, Gilani Research Foundation, 22 September 2014.
'NATO publics blame Russia for Ukrainian Crisis, but reluctant to provide military aid', Pew Research Center, 10 June 2015.

## Journal Articles

Dicey Edward, 'The Unionist vote', *The Nineteenth Century*, July–December 1886.
'British Institute of Public Opinion', *Public Opinion Quarterly*, 1940, pp. 77–78.
'Gallup and Fortune Polls: British Reactions', *Public Opinion Quarterly*, 1941, p. 157.
'Gallup and Fortune Polls: British Reactions', *Public Opinion Quarterly*, 1943, p. 330.
'In Britain', *Public Opinion Quarterly*, 1944, p. 294.
Hazel Erskine, 'The polls: is war a mistake?' *Public Opinion Quarterly*, 1970–71, p. 135.
Elie Kedourie, 'Arab political memoirs', *Encounter*, November 1972, pp. 70–83.
Paul Hollander, 'The Ideological Pilgrim', *Encounter*, November 1973.
Colin Clark, 'The "Golden Age" of the Great Economists: Keynes, Robbins et al. in 1930', *Encounter*, June 1977.
B. J. Elliott, 'The League of Nations Union and History Teaching in England: A Study in Benevolent Bias', *History of Education*, 1977, pp. 131–141.
Michael Howard, '"Many reasons" for Vietnam', *Encounter*, May 1979, p. 24.
Robert W. Oldendick and Barbara Ann Bardes, 'Mass and elite foreign policy opinions', *Public Opinion Quarterly*, February 1982, pp. 368–381.
Tom W. Smith, 'The polls- A Report: Nuclear Anxiety', *Public Opinion Quarterly*, Winter 1988b, p. 563.
Peter C Gronn, 'An experiment in political education; "V.G.", "Slimy" and the Repton Sixth, 1916–1918', *History of Education*, 1990, pp. 1–21.

Timothy Garton Ash, 'Bosnia in Our Future', *New York Review of Books*, 21 December 1995.
Robert D. Kaplan reply to Timothy Garton Ash, *New York Review of Books*, 21 March 1996.
Bernadotte C. Hayes and Ian McAllister, 'Public support for political violence and paramilitaries in Northern Ireland the Republic of Ireland', *Terrorism and Political Violence*, 12/2005, Volume 17.
Maria Rose Rublee, 'Fantasy Counterfactual: A Nuclear-Armed Ukraine', *Survival*, April-May 2015, p. 145.
Mike Clarke, 'The ending of wars and the ending of eras', *RUSI Journal*, August/September 2015.

## SELECT NEWSPAPER ARTICLES

'Massacre haunts modern India', *The Guardian*, 13 April 1987.
Karan Thapa, 'Myths of the Raj', *The Times*, 31 December 1987.
Bernard Levin, 'Stalin's authorised massacre', *The Times*, 13 April 1993.
'Queen to say sorry to Maori people', *The Independent*, 2 July 1995.
'Iceland finally warms to its Cold War Role', *The Times*, 16 February 1999.
'Resurrection of a patriot?' *The Hindu*, 23 January, 2000.
'North Korea apologises to Japan for bizarre tale of kidnap and intrigue', *The Guardian*, 18 September 2002.
'How he lost it', *The Hindu*, 4 September 2005.
'NDTV poll: icons from Mahatma Gandhi to Sachin', *The Hindu*, 12 August 2007.
Simon Sebag Montefiori, 'Is the greatest Russian Stalin or Nicholas? The answer is obvious', *The Times*, 18 July 2008.
'At last, Stalin is defeated by voters', *The Times*, 29 December 2008.
'"Assumptions not evidence" led Blair into Iraq War', *The Times*, 19 January 2010.
'Doctors go to court for inquest on David Kelly', *The Times*, 4 September 2010.
'Al-Qaeda pogrom may drive last Christians from the country', *The Times*, 11 November 2010.
'The faithful who must choose to walk in the shadow of death', *The Times*, 20 December 2010.
'Pope Francis criticised Britain over Falkland islands', *Time World*, 14 March 2013.
'Hamid Karzai's latest outburst at NATO is a sign of his deep frustration', *The Guardian*, 8 October 2013.
'India helping in having our own army: Karzai', *The Hindu*, Madras, 15 December 2013.
'Most Christians flee after jihadist ultimatum', *The Hindu*, 20 July 2014.

'Teaching History: Chapter 10 in which democracies join in East Asia's history wars', *The Economist*, 5 July 2014, p. 52.
'Americans neutral on Taiwan', *Taipei Times*, 18 September 2014.
'How education makes people less religious—and less superstitious too', *The Economist*, 11 October 2014, p. 73.
'Japan retreats from sex slave apology', *The Times*, 17 October 2014.
'The Editor who toppled Nixon', *The Economist*, 25 October 2014, p. 49.
'The President's Stargazer: Joan Quigley, astrologer to the Reagans died on October 22, aged 87', *The Economist*, 8 November 2014, p. 98.
'Japan and the War: Abe's demons', *The Economist*, 6 December 2014.
'British Elections Other Losers: Pollsters', *New York Times*, 8 May 2015.
'Dictators join Putin's victory parade', *Sunday Times*, 10 May 2015.
'Road kill', *The Economist*, 4 July 2015, p. 31.
'In victory for Philippines, Hague Court to hear dispute over South China Sea', *New York Times*, 30 October 2015.
Nigel Biggar, 'Japan's face-saving still poisons the world', *The Times*, 16 February 2016.

## Selected Downloaded Material

'Canadian Government apologizes for abuse of indigenous people', http://articles.washingtonpost.com/2008-06-12/world
'Kevin Rudd's sorry speech', 13 February 2008 in http://www.smh.com.au/articles/2008/02/13
'Blair "sorry" for UK slavery role', BBC News Channel, 14 March 2007, http://news.bbc.co.uk
'US admiral reassures Philippines of help in disputed sea', http://www.voanews.com/content/reu-us-admiral 17 February 2014.
Sugiura Masaaki, 'Revising the Kono statement carries Japan-South Korea relations into unknown water', Japan Forum on International Relations, E Letter 20 April 2014, Volume 7, number 2.
'When people of faith lose the ability to live peacefully together', BBC Thought for the Day, 20 June 2014, website of Lord Sachs.
'Taipei mayor's comments on benefits of colonisation draw rebukes', 25 January 2015, http://focustaiwan.tw/news/aall/201501310021.aspx
Jennifer Lind, 'Apologies in international politics', *Security Studies*, 18:3, 517–556, DO1.1080/09636410903132987.

# INDEX

**A**
Abe, Shinzo
  and World War, 11
Aboriginal people apologies to, 10
Afghanistan
  and British interventions in the 19th Century, 94
  and US intervention in 2001, 91
Airpower and guerrillas, 95–96
  in Bosnia, 91
Albright, Madeleine
  apologises for bombing of Chinese Embassy, 26
  on intervention, 90
Amritsar massacre and apologies, 57, 59
Argentine opinion and Falklands War, 79
Armed forces professionalisation, 27
Armenian demand for Turkish apology, 62
Astrology and prophecy, 105
Australian apology to aborigines, 60

**B**
Balfour Declaration on Jewish Homeland, 80
Balkan wars, 13–14
Banks fined for malpractice, 58
Barnett, Correlli
  prophecy and Soviet collapse, 110
Barton, Keith
  and Northern Irish education, 68
Best, George
  as hero, 28
Black people and US history teaching, 70–71
Blumenfeld, Laura and Palestinians, 40
Boer War British guilt, 24
Bomber offensive British views of, 33
Bosnian intervention, 32
  and British intervention in Sierra Leone and Afghanistan, 93–94
War, 91
British opinion and war, 33–34
Bush, George H.W.
  and Iraq in 1990, 89–90
Bush, George W.
  and international affairs, 97
  orders invasion of Afghanistan, 91

## C

Canada popularity of, 30
  apology to indigenous people, 60
Carr E.H.
  predictions, 109
Children and politics, 68
China and Japan, 52–53
  hatred of US during Korean War, 45
  settles borders with neighbours, 133–134
  in South China Sea, 133
  unpopularity, 30
Civilians in wartime, 2, 4, 10
Collective punishment, 58
Collins, Eamon
  and IRA, 40
Communist brutality 116–118
Conference on Security and Co-operation in Europe, 1973-5, 61, 132
Crusades, 17

## D

Destabilisation and defeat, 107
Diana Princess as national heroine, 28–29
Disease and casualties, 22
Djilas, Milovan
  and Balkan wars, 14
Dorman, Andrew
  and Sierra Leone intervention, 93
Duty to protect, 88
Dyer, Reginald
  and Amritsar massacre, 57

## E

Elite opinion in Britain 34
Enclosures 18th Century 52
English people and their history, 9

European states refugees and terrorists, 135

## F

Falkland Islands Argentine claim, 79
Films and suffering, 29
First World War casualties, 22
Force use of and unpopularity, 31–32
Franco-US relations, 42
French history teaching after First World War, 69

## G

Gaza, Israeli bombardment of, 31
German army and Nazism, 58
German conditions in 1945, 40
Germans expelled from Eastern Europe, 80–81
Good Friday Agreement, 16
Gorbachev, Mikhail, 110
Great Leap Forward, 13, 59

## H

Haldane, Aylmer
  and Iraq in 1919, 94
Harper, Stephen
  apology to indigenous people, 60
Heroes, modern, 28
Hinsley, F.H.
  predictions, 109
Hiroshima, 1
  and British, 12
Historical ignorance, 27
History and predictions, 104, 108
History teaching, 69
Hitler, Adolf
  and 1919 Peace Settlement, 3
Holocaust, 23, 59

INDEX 157

Hostages in Teheran Pakistani attitudes towards, 31
Howard, Michael
 and Vietnam War, 89

**I**
Influenza pandemic, 22
Intellectuals and war, 128
Intervention by the West, 87–90, 98
Iraqi invasion of Kuwait, 16
Iraq uprising 1919, 94
 unpopularity of 2003 invasion, 32
Iraq War and British army, 57
IRA victims, 34
Irish hostility to Britain, 15–16
Irish nationalism, 15
Irish potato famine, Tony Blair apologises for, 55–56
Islam and West, 17
Islamic State unpopularity, 30
Israeli attitudes to war, 32
 history teaching, 71

**J**
Japan and history teaching, 71–72
Japan nuclear attack, 1, 10–11
 apologies for war, 54
Japanese motives for war, 11
Jewish population in Palestine 1940s, 80
John Paul (Pope)
 and apologies, 59
Just war and collective responsibility, 58

**K**
Kagan, Roger
 and US attitudes to war, 31
Karadzic, Radovan, 96

Katyn massacre of Poles, 116
Kennedy, John
 remembered, 28
Kennedy, Paul
 and weaknesses of US, 129
Kidnap by North Koreans of Japanese, 54–55
Kuwait invaded by Iraq, 89

**L**
Law of Sea Treaty and South China Sea, 133–134
Leaders and apologies, 56
Lennon John assassination, 28
Lloyd, Selwyn
 and Suez operation, 56

**M**
Major, John
 and Iraq in 1991, 90
Malta and George Cross, 40
McLaren, Moray Anglo-Scottish relations, 16–17
Media and war, 21–23, 88
 bad news, 128
 focus on disaster, 26
Memory, 2, 4, 10
 and prediction, 104–105
Military power fear of, 29–30
Military professionalisation, 26
Miller, Hugh
 and Anglo-Scottish relations, 16
Morgenthau, Henry
 and Armenians, 62
Motives, 3
 for war British, 32

**N**
Napoleon speech before Borodino, 25

Nationalism in Balkans, 13–14
Nazi brutality, 116–118
Nelson, Horatio
  as hero, 27
New Zealand apology to Maoris, 60
Northern Irish history teaching, 68–69
Novelty popularity of, 128
Nuclear Non-Proliferation Treaty, 132
Nuclear weapons flaunted by Russia and China, 131
  made safe in Russia, 131
  removed from Ukraine, 131

O
Obama, Barak
  and military power, 92
  popularity, 30

P
Pakistan and India since independence, 109–110
  and outside interference, 10
Palestinian-Israeli hostility, 79–83
Paris Peace Conference 1919 and territorial settlement, 78–79
Partition peaceful of countries, 78
Pew polls, 2
Picts destroyed, 9
Pinochet, Augusto trial, 43
Poets and War, 25
Popularity of countries survey, 30
Potato famine, 15
Powell, Colin
  and intervention, 90
Powell, Jonathan
  and Iraqi weapons of mass destruction, 106
Pride in European country, 16
Prisoners of war and Japanese, 33

Prophesies Delphi, 105
Putin, Vladimir
  popularity in Russia, 133

R
Race, Jeffrey
  and Vietnam War, 88
Rahman, Abdur (Emir of Afghanistan), 94
Reagan, Ronald
  and astrology, 105
Red Guards in China, 41
Remembrance Sunday, 28
Reporting on wars, 23–26
Revolutions and military power, 108
Rudd, Kevin
  apology to aborigines, 60
Russell, W.H.
  and Crimean War, 24
Russia, China and victimisation, 131
Russia invasions of, 106–107, 131
Russian nuclear weapons made safe, 44

S
Sadat Anwar speech in Israeli Parliament, 79
Saddam Hussein overthrown, 30
Scottish nationalism, 16–17
Sedan, siege of 24
Shah of Iran abandoned by West, 43
Sierra Leone, British intervention in, 32
Sino-Japanese War, 2–3, 11
Slavery, 9–10
Slave trade Blair, apology for, 56
Soldiers and racing drivers, 26
Soviet military in World War, 11, 131
Spear Perceval predictions, 109
Statue of Liberty, 42
Statues of heroes and heroines, 27

Straw, Jack
  and Iraq invasion, 57
Suez Crisis and British apologies, 56
Suicide bombers, 26
  casualties from, 22
Syrians massacre of Assyrians, 42

**T**
Taiwan and end of Second World War, 11
  celebrations 2015, 11
  Chinese claims to, 83
Tennyson, Alfred
  and war, 25
Terror casualties from, 22
Thomson, David
  and Irish, 15
Trade and its effects, 130
Trevelyan, Charles
  and Irish potato famine, 15
Trevelyan G.M.
  and prediction 111
Trump, Donald
  career and policies, 129–139
  elected president, 110–111
  and US public, 92
  on US victimisation, 32
Turkey and apology for Armenians, 62
Twin Towers attack, 91–92
Twitter, 129

**U**
Ukraine and CSCE 1994, 132
UN Special Session on Disarmament 1978, 1

US aircraft losses in Vietnam War, 95
  overseas bases and colonialism, 72
  position in the world, 129–130
  Presidential election 2016, 3, 126–129
  public opinion and war, 92
US, Britain and victimisation, 32–33

**V**
Victims Jews, aboriginal people, 29
Vietnam War and US history texts, 72–73
  culture, 88

**W**
War 'lessons,' 90
Wellington, Duke and occupation of France in 1815, 90
West, Rebecca
  and Balkans, 14
Winter, Jay
  and wartime suffering, 24
Women as soldiers, 26
World Peace Day, 1
World War, 2
  suffering, 22–23

**Y**
Yugoslav collapse, 14
  civil war, 96
  resistance to the Nazis, 95